THE ULTIMATE GUIDE TO SOCIAL MEDIA MARKETING:

Strategies for Success

I0427276

RUSTY HUNT

TABLE OF CONTENTS

Chapter 1: Introduction to Social Media Marketing......1

The Importance of Social Media Marketing.................2

The Evolution of Social Media Platforms......................3

Understanding the Target Audience
in Social Media Marketing 7

**Chapter 2: Creating a Social Media Marketing
Strategy 10**

Setting Clear Goals and Objectives.............................11

Defining Target Audience and Buyer Personas 13

Choosing the Right Social Media Platforms...............15

Content Creation and Curation 18

Scheduling and Posting Strategies..............................20

Chapter 3: Building a Strong Social Media Presence .23

Creating Compelling Profiles and Bios.......................24

Designing Engaging Visuals and Branding 26

Increasing Followers and Engagement 29

Utilizing Hashtags and Trending Topics.....................31

Chapter 4: Content Marketing on Social Media..........33

Creating High-Quality and Valuable Content............34

Understanding Different Types of Content.................36

Implementing Content Strategy and Planning............39

Leveraging User-Generated Content 41

Analyzing and Optimizing Content Performance.......43

Chapter 5: Advertising and Promotion on Social Media 45

Introduction to Social Media Advertising 46

Choosing the Right Ad Formats and Objectives 49

Targeting and Retargeting Strategies 52

Budgeting and Bidding in Social Media Advertising .. 54

Tracking and Measuring Ad Performance 56

Chapter 6: Influencer Marketing and Partnerships 59

Understanding Influencer Marketing 60

Researching and Identifying Relevant Influencers 62

Building Relationships and Negotiating Partnerships . 65

Creating Effective Influencer Campaigns 68

Measuring the Success of Influencer Marketing 70

Chapter 7: Social Media Analytics and Reporting 72

Importance of Analytics in Social Media Marketing ... 73

Tracking Key Performance Indicators (KPIs) 74

Analyzing Reach, Engagement, and Conversion 77

Tools and Platforms for Social Media Analytics 80

Creating Comprehensive Reports and Insights 82

Chapter 8: Social Media Crisis Management 84

Identifying and Responding to Potential Crises 85

Developing a Crisis Management Plan 87

Handling Negative Feedback and Trolls 89

Rebuilding Reputation and Trust 92

Learning from Crisis Situations 95

Chapter 9: Future Trends and Innovations in Social Media Marketing 98

Emerging Social Media Platforms and Features 99

Artificial Intelligence and Chatbots in Marketing......101

Video Marketing and Live Streaming 103

Virtual Reality (VR) and Augmented Reality (AR) 107

The Future of Social Media Marketing..................... 109

Chapter 10: Conclusion and Final Thoughts.............. 112

Recap of Key Strategies and Techniques....................113

Implementing and Iterating
Social Media Marketing Plans.....................................115

Continuous Learning and Staying Updated...............117

Success Stories and Case Studies 120

Final Words and Encouragement
for Social Media Marketers 123

CHAPTER 1

INTRODUCTION TO SOCIAL MEDIA MARKETING

THE IMPORTANCE OF SOCIAL MEDIA MARKETING

In today's digital age, social media has become an integral part of our daily lives. With billions of people actively engaging on various platforms, it has transformed the way businesses connect with their target audience. In this sub-chapter, we will explore the importance of social media marketing and how it can revolutionize your marketing and advertising strategies.

Social media marketing offers unparalleled opportunities for businesses to engage with their customers, build brand awareness, and drive sales. Unlike traditional marketing channels, social media allows for direct interaction and real-time engagement. It fosters a two-way communication channel, enabling businesses to listen to their audience, address their concerns, and provide personalized solutions. By actively participating on social media platforms, businesses can establish themselves as thought leaders, gain trust, and build long-term relationships with their customers.

One of the key advantages of social media marketing is its cost-effectiveness.

Compared to traditional advertising methods, social media platforms offer affordable advertising options that can reach a large and highly targeted audience. With advanced targeting capabilities, businesses can narrow down their audience based on demographics, interests, and behaviors, ensuring that their message reaches the right people at the right time. This level of precision targeting maximizes the return on investment and offers measurable results.

Furthermore, social media marketing allows businesses to gather valuable insights and data about their audience. With the help of analytics tools, marketers can track engagement, measure campaign performance, and gain deep insights into customer behavior. This data-driven approach empowers businesses to refine their strategies, optimize their content, and make informed decisions to drive their marketing efforts forward.

Another significant advantage of social media marketing is its ability to create viral content. By creating engaging and shareable content, businesses can tap into the power of social sharing, potentially reaching millions of users within seconds. This viral nature of social media amplifies brand exposure, increases brand awareness, and generates organic traffic.

In conclusion, social media marketing is an essential component of any marketing and advertising strategy. Its ability to connect businesses with their target audience, its cost-effectiveness, data-driven approach, and potential for virality make it a powerful tool for success. By embracing social media marketing, businesses can stay ahead of the competition, build brand loyalty, and drive growth in the digital landscape.

THE EVOLUTION OF SOCIAL MEDIA PLATFORMS

In today's fast-paced digital age, social media has become an integral part of our daily lives. From connecting with friends and family to sharing our thoughts, experiences, and content, social media platforms have revolutionized the way we communicate and interact with the world. This sub-chapter will delve into the fascinating evolution of social media platforms, exploring their inception, growth, and the impact they have had on the field of marketing and advertising.

The journey of social media platforms began in the early s with the emergence of platforms like Friendster and MySpace. These early platforms allowed users to create profiles, connect with friends, and share content. However, they were limited in terms of functionality and user experience.

The turning point came with the launch of Facebook in 2004, which completely transformed the social media landscape. With its clean interface, user-friendly features, and focus on connecting people, Facebook quickly

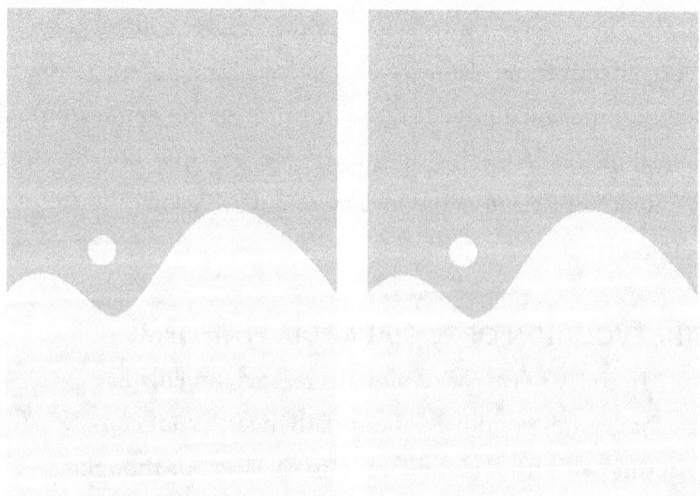

gained popularity and became the go-to platform for social interaction.

Its advertising potential was soon realized, leading to the birth of social media marketing as a powerful tool for businesses to reach their target audience.

As Facebook continued to dominate the social media scene, other platforms like Twitter, LinkedIn, and YouTube entered the market, each offering unique features and catering to different niches. Twitter allowed for real-time communication through short messages, LinkedIn became the professional networking hub, and YouTube revolutionized video sharing.

The rise of smartphones and the advent of mobile apps further propelled the evolution of social media platforms. Platforms like Instagram and Snapchat capitalized on the trend of visual content, enabling users to share photos and videos instantly. Their success demonstrated the

growing importance of visual storytelling in marketing and advertising.

In recent years, we have witnessed the emergence of new platforms such as TikTok and Clubhouse, which have gained immense popularity, particularly among younger audiences. These platforms have introduced innovative features and formats, showcasing the ever-evolving nature of social media.

The evolution of social media platforms has had a profound impact on marketing and advertising. Businesses now have the opportunity to reach a wider audience, engage with them on a personal level, and build brand loyalty. The targeted advertising capabilities offered by social media platforms allow marketers to tailor their messages to specific demographics, maximizing their return on investment.

As social media platforms continue to evolve, marketers and advertisers must stay updated with the latest trends and adapt their strategies accordingly.

Understanding the history and evolution of these platforms is crucial to effectively navigate the dynamic landscape of social media marketing.

In conclusion, the evolution of social media platforms has revolutionized the way we communicate, connect, and market our products and services. From the early days of Friendster to the current dominance of platforms like Facebook, Twitter, and Instagram, each platform has contributed to the ever-expanding world of social media marketing. By understanding the history and evolution of these platforms, marketers and advertisers can stay ahead of the curve and leverage the power of social media to achieve success in their campaigns.

UNDERSTANDING THE TARGET AUDIENCE IN SOCIAL MEDIA MARKETING

In the ever-evolving landscape of social media marketing, one thing remains constant: understanding your target

audience is the key to success. Whether you are a seasoned marketer or someone new to the field, comprehending the intricacies of your target audience is crucial for developing effective strategies that yield tangible results. This subchapter will delve into the importance of understanding your target audience in social media marketing and provide actionable insights to help you reach your marketing goals.

For anyone in marketing and/or advertising, and particularly those in the niche of social media marketing, knowing your target audience goes beyond demographics and basic user profiles. It requires a deep understanding of their preferences, behaviors, and motivations. By gaining insights into your audience's needs and desires, you can tailor your marketing efforts to resonate with them on a personal level.

One effective way to understand your target audience is by conducting thorough market research. This involves analyzing data from various sources, such as social media analytics, customer surveys, and competitor analysis. By leveraging this information, you can identify your audience's interests, pain points, and online behavior patterns. This knowledge will empower you to create content that speaks directly to your target audience, increasing engagement and driving conversions.

Furthermore, understanding your target audience helps you choose the right social media platforms to focus your marketing efforts on. Different demographics tend to favor specific platforms, and being aware of these preferences allows you to allocate your resources effectively. For instance, if your audience consists primarily of young adults, platforms like Instagram and TikTok might be more suitable for reaching and engaging with them. On the other hand, if your target audience comprises professionals and corporate entities, LinkedIn may be the ideal platform to showcase your brand and content.

In conclusion, understanding your target audience is the cornerstone of successful social media marketing. By investing time and effort into researching and comprehending your audience's preferences, behaviors, and motivations, you can develop tailored marketing strategies that resonate with them. This subchapter has provided valuable insights to guide you on this journey, helping you unlock the full potential of your social media marketing efforts.

CREATING A SOCIAL MEDIA MARKETING STRATEGY

SETTING CLEAR GOALS AND OBJECTIVES

In the fast-paced world of social media marketing, it is crucial for marketers and advertisers to set clear goals and objectives. Without a clear roadmap, it is easy to get lost in the ever-changing landscape of social media platforms and strategies. This subchapter will delve into the importance of setting clear goals and objectives, and provide practical tips on how to do so effectively.

Why are clear goals and objectives important in social media marketing? Simply put, they provide direction and purpose to your marketing efforts. They help you define what you want to achieve and how you will measure success. Without clear goals, it becomes difficult to determine whether your social media marketing efforts are effective or not.

The first step in setting clear goals and objectives is to identify what you hope to achieve through your social media marketing efforts. Are you looking to increase brand awareness, generate leads, drive website traffic, or boost

sales? Each goal requires a different approach and metrics to measure success. By identifying your goals upfront, you can tailor your strategies and tactics accordingly.

Once you have identified your goals, it is essential to make them specific, measurable, attainable, relevant, and time-bound (SMART). This framework ensures that your goals are realistic and actionable. For example, instead of setting a vague goal like "increase brand awareness," a SMART goal could be "increase brand awareness by 20% in six months through targeted social media campaigns."

In addition to setting goals, it is equally important to define clear objectives. Objectives are the specific steps or milestones that will help you achieve your goals. They provide a roadmap for your social media marketing efforts. For instance, if your goal is to drive website traffic, your objectives could include increasing organic reach, improving click-through rates, or optimizing landing pages.

To effectively set clear goals and objectives, it is essential to regularly track and analyze your social media metrics. This data will help you measure your progress, identify areas for improvement, and make data- driven decisions. Tools like Google Analytics, social media analytics, and customer feedback can provide valuable insights into the effectiveness of your strategies.

In conclusion, setting clear goals and objectives is vital for anyone in marketing and/or advertising, particularly in the niche of social media marketing. By defining your goals upfront, making them SMART, and setting clear objectives, you can create a roadmap for success in the ever-evolving world of social media marketing. Regularly tracking and analyzing metrics will ensure that you stay on track and make data-driven decisions to achieve your desired outcomes.

DEFINING TARGET AUDIENCE AND BUYER PERSONAS

In the ever-evolving landscape of social media marketing, understanding your target audience and creating buyer personas are essential steps towards achieving success. Whether you are a seasoned marketer or new to the world of advertising, identifying and defining your target audience is crucial for effective social media campaigns.

This subchapter aims to provide you with a comprehensive guide on how to define your target audience and create buyer personas tailored to the niche of social media marketing.

To begin, let's clarify the importance of defining your target audience.

Social media platforms offer a vast audience, but not every user will be interested in your products or services. By narrowing down your target audience, you can focus your efforts on reaching those most likely to engage with your brand, resulting in higher conversion rates and better return on investment.

To define your target audience, start by conducting thorough market research. Analyze demographics, psychographics, and behavioral patterns to gain insights into who your potential customers are and what motivates them. Utilize social media analytics tools to gather data on user behavior, interests, and preferences. This information will help you identify common characteristics among your target audience and segment them accordingly.

Once you have defined your target audience, creating buyer personas can further refine your marketing strategy. Buyer personas are fictional representations of your ideal customers, based on real data and educated assumptions. They go beyond basic demographic information and delve into the motivations, goals, challenges, and preferences of your target audience.

To create effective buyer personas, start by identifying key demographic factors such as age, gender, location, and occupation. Then, explore their psychographic traits, including their interests, values, beliefs, and aspirations. Consider their pain points and challenges that your products or services can address. Additionally, understand their preferred social media platforms, communication styles, and content consumption habits.

By developing detailed buyer personas, you can tailor your social media marketing efforts to resonate with your target audience on a deeper level. Craft compelling content, personalized ads, and engaging campaigns that align with their interests and needs. This will not only attract their attention but also establish trust and credibility with your brand.

In conclusion, defining your target audience and creating buyer personas are fundamental steps in social media marketing. By understanding who you are targeting and what motivates them, you can develop strategies that effectively engage and convert your ideal customers. Continuously reassess and refine your personas as the market evolves to ensure your social media marketing efforts remain relevant and impactful.

CHOOSING THE RIGHT SOCIAL MEDIA PLATFORMS

In today's digital age, social media has become an integral part of any marketing and advertising strategy.

With millions of active users on various social media platforms, it has become crucial for businesses to establish a strong online presence. However, not all social media platforms are created equal, and determining which ones are the most effective for your specific marketing goals is essential.

When it comes to choosing the right social media platforms, it's important to consider factors such as your target audience, the nature of your business, and the type of content you plan to share. Each social media platform has its own unique features and characteristics, making it suitable for specific niches and marketing strategies.

One of the most popular social media platforms is Facebook. With over 2.8 billion monthly active users, it provides a vast audience for businesses to connect with. Facebook is ideal for businesses targeting a wide range of demographics, as it offers various ad formats and targeting options. Additionally, Facebook's detailed analytics can help you track the performance of your campaigns and make data-driven decisions.

For businesses focusing on visual content, Instagram is a great platform to consider. With over 1 billion monthly active users, it has become a hub for influencers and brand collaborations.

Instagram's visually appealing nature makes it perfect for showcasing products, lifestyle content, and behind-the-scenes glimpses. Utilizing features such as Instagram Stories and IGTV can help you engage with your audience on a more personal level.

LinkedIn, on the other hand, is a professional networking platform that caters to B B marketing. With over 740 million users, it provides an ideal space for businesses to establish thought

leadership, connect with industry professionals, and share valuable content.

LinkedIn's advertising options, such as Sponsored Content and InMail, allow businesses to target specific professional demographics effectively.

Twitter, known for its real-time nature, is suitable for businesses that thrive on providing instant updates and engaging in conversations. With 330 million monthly active users, it offers a platform for businesses to monitor trends, participate in industry discussions, and engage with their audience through concise messaging.

When choosing the right social media platforms

for your marketing strategy, it's crucial to evaluate your goals, target audience, and the strengths of each platform. A thorough understanding of your niche and the specific features of each platform will enable you to maximize your social media marketing efforts and achieve success in your campaigns. Remember, it's not just about being present on every platform, but about selecting the ones that align with your brand, resonate with your audience, and drive meaningful engagement.

CONTENT CREATION AND CURATION

In the fast-paced world of social media marketing, staying relevant and engaging with your target audience is paramount. To achieve this, content creation and curation play a pivotal role in building a successful social media strategy. This subchapter will delve into the importance of content creation and curation, providing valuable insights

and practical tips for anyone in marketing and/or advertising within the niche of social media marketing.

Creating compelling and original content is the foundation of any successful social media marketing campaign. By crafting unique and relevant content, you can capture the attention of your audience, increase brand awareness, and drive engagement. This subchapter will guide you through the process of creating high-quality content, from conducting thorough research to understanding your audience's preferences and needs. You will learn how to develop a content calendar, select the most appropriate content formats, and optimize your content for different social media platforms.

However, content creation is not the only key to success in social media marketing. Curating content from external sources can also be a valuable strategy to augment your brand's online presence. By sharing relevant and interesting content from reputable sources, you position yourself as a trusted industry expert and provide your audience with valuable insights. This subchapter will explore the art of content curation, including how to identify trustworthy sources, effectively curate content, and attribute credit to the original creators.

Furthermore, this subchapter will also address the importance of maintaining a balance between content creation and curation. Finding the right mix will enable you to consistently provide fresh and engaging content, while also leveraging the expertise of others to enhance your brand's authority. You will learn how to strike this balance and develop a content strategy that aligns with your marketing goals and resonates with your audience.

In conclusion, content creation and curation are fundamental aspects of social media marketing. By incorporating these strategies into your overall marketing plan, you can establish a strong online presence, build brand loyalty, and drive meaningful engagement with your target audience. Whether you are a seasoned marketer or just starting in the field, this subchapter will equip you with the knowledge and tools to create and curate compelling content that sets you apart in the competitive landscape of social media marketing.

SCHEDULING AND POSTING STRATEGIES

In the fast-paced world of social media marketing, it is crucial to have effective scheduling and posting strategies in place. This subchapter will delve into the best practices and strategies for scheduling and posting on social media platforms, ensuring that your marketing efforts yield the desired results.

Timing is everything when it comes to social media marketing. Knowing when to post your content can significantly impact its reach and engagement.

Understanding your audience's online behavior and the optimal times they are active on various platforms is essential. By utilizing analytics tools and studying your target audience's behavior patterns, you can determine the perfect time to schedule your posts. This not only ensures maximum visibility but also increases the chances of your content being shared and commented on.

Consistency is key in social media marketing. Developing a consistent posting schedule helps build trust and reliability with your audience. Create a content calendar that outlines the frequency and timing of your posts across different platforms. It is crucial to strike a balance between posting too frequently, which may overwhelm your audience, and posting too sparingly, which may lead to a loss of interest. Experiment with different posting frequencies and analyze the engagement metrics to find the sweet spot for each platform you use.

In addition to timing and consistency, content quality is paramount. Craft compelling and visually appealing posts that resonate with your target audience. Use a mix of text, images, videos, and infographics to keep your content diverse and engaging. Tailor your posts to each social media platform, considering the preferred content formats and user demographics. Experiment with different types of content and analyze the engagement levels to identify what resonates best with your audience.

Automation tools can be a game-changer in streamlining your scheduling and posting strategies. Platforms like Hootsuite, Buffer, and Sprout Social allow you to schedule posts in advance, saving you time and effort. Take advantage of these tools to plan your content calendar weeks or even months in advance, ensuring a consistent presence on social media.

In conclusion, effective scheduling and posting strategies are crucial for successful social media marketing. By understanding your audience, determining optimal posting times, maintaining consistency, and focusing on content quality, you can maximize your reach and engagement on social media platforms. Utilize automation tools to streamline your efforts and save time, ultimately leading to greater success in your social media marketing endeavors.

CHAPTER 3

BUILDING A STRONG
SOCIAL MEDIA PRESENCE

CREATING COMPELLING PROFILES AND BIOS

In the fast-paced world of social media marketing, having a compelling profile and bio is crucial to capturing the attention of your audience. Your profile and bio serve as the first impression for potential customers, so it's essential to make them count. This subchapter will guide you through the process of creating profiles and bios that are engaging, authentic, and representative of your brand.

1. Understanding Your Audience:

    Before crafting your profiles and bios, it's important to have a deep understanding of your target audience. Research their demographics, interests, and pain points. This knowledge will help you tailor your messaging and ensure that your profiles resonate with your audience.

2. Consistency Across Platforms:

    Consistency is key when it comes to branding. Your profiles and bios should reflect your brand's

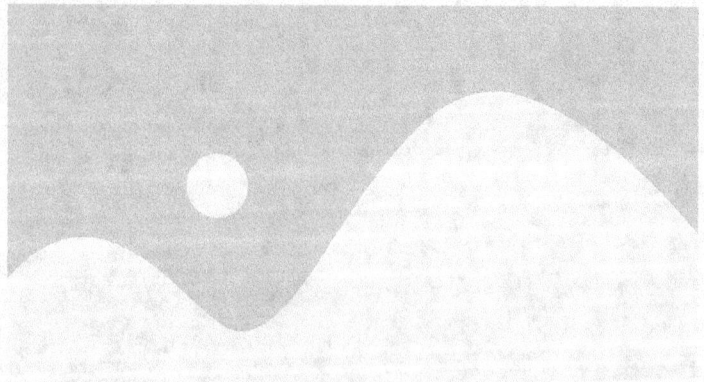

voice, values, and aesthetics consistently across all social media platforms. This will create a cohesive and recognizable brand identity that your audience can trust.

3. Showcasing Your Expertise:

   Use your profiles and bios to establish yourself as an authority in your niche. Highlight your accomplishments, credentials, and relevant experience to build credibility and trust. Share success stories and testimonials to demonstrate your expertise and the value you bring to your audience.

4. Crafting an Engaging Bio:

   Your bio should be concise, attention- grabbing, and showcase your unique selling proposition. It should communicate what sets you apart from your competitors and why your audience should choose you. Use keywords that are relevant to your niche to optimize your bio for search engines and attract the right audience.

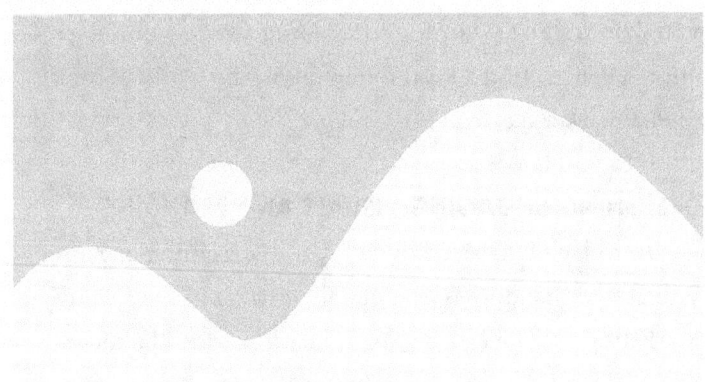

5. Adding a Personal Touch:

   While it's important to maintain a professional tone, injecting a personal touch into your profiles and bios can help humanize your brand. Share personal anecdotes or stories that relate to your brand's values or mission. This will create an emotional connection with your audience and make your brand more relatable.

6. Utilizing Visuals:

   Incorporate visuals such as high- quality profile pictures, cover photos, and graphics that are consistent with your brand's aesthetics. Visuals can capture attention and make your profiles more visually appealing, increasing the likelihood of engagement from your audience.

Remember, creating compelling profiles and bios is an ongoing process. Continually update and refine them based on feedback, analytics, and emerging trends. By investing time and effort into crafting engaging profiles and bios, you'll be well on your way to building a strong online presence and attracting a loyal following in the world of social media marketing.

DESIGNING ENGAGING VISUALS AND BRANDING

In today's fast-paced digital world, designing engaging visuals and branding is essential for anyone in the field of marketing and advertising, particularly within the niche of social media marketing. With millions of posts competing for attention on various social media platforms, it

has become increasingly challenging to capture the interest of users.

However, by incorporating visually appealing graphics and consistent branding elements, marketers can effectively grab attention, convey their message, and establish a strong brand presence.

Visuals play a crucial role in social media marketing as they have the power to evoke emotions, tell stories, and leave a lasting impact on the audience.

Incorporating eye-catching images, videos, and infographics can instantly capture the attention of users scrolling through their social media feeds. Additionally, using visually appealing content that aligns with the brand's message helps to create a sense of consistency and professionalism, ultimately enhancing brand credibility.

When it comes to designing engaging visuals, it is essential to understand the target audience and tailor the content accordingly. By conducting thorough market research and understanding the demographics, interests, and preferences of the target audience, marketers can create visuals that resonate with their viewers. Whether it is through the use of vibrant colors, captivating typography, or relatable imagery, the key is to create an emotional connection with the audience.

Furthermore, branding is crucial in social media marketing as it helps to differentiate a brand from its competitors and build recognition. Consistency in branding elements such as logos, color schemes, and typography across all social media platforms is vital for creating a cohesive brand identity. This consistency builds trust and familiarity among the audience, making it easier for them to recognize and engage with the brand's content.

However, designing engaging visuals and branding is not just about aesthetics; it is also about functionality. Marketers should ensure that their visuals are optimized for various social media platforms, taking into consideration the image dimensions and file sizes. By adapting visuals to t the requirements of different platforms, marketers can ensure that their content appears professional and visually appealing across all social media channels.

In conclusion, designing engaging visuals and branding is a critical component of successful social media marketing. By incorporating visually appealing graphics, tailoring content to the target audience, and maintaining consistency in branding elements, marketers can effectively capture the attention of users, convey their message, and establish a strong brand presence in the competitive world of social media marketing.

INCREASING FOLLOWERS AND ENGAGEMENT

In today's digital age, social media marketing has become an indispensable tool for anyone in marketing and advertising. With the power to reach millions of potential customers, social media platforms offer a unique opportunity to promote your brand, increase your followers, and boost engagement. This subchapter in "The Ultimate Guide to Social Media Marketing: Strategies for Success" delves into the key strategies and techniques to excel in the realm of social media marketing, catering to individuals focused on the niche of Social Media Marketing.

Building a substantial following on social media is crucial for success. The larger your audience, the more eyes you have on your content, and the greater your chances of converting followers into loyal customers. This subchapter offers expert insights into various strategies to increase your followers organically. From optimizing your social media profiles to creating compelling and shareable content, you'll discover the precise steps required to attract followers who resonate with your brand and are genuinely interested in what you have to offer.

However, having a massive following alone is not enough. It is equally important to drive engagement and cultivate a community around your brand. This subchapter goes beyond

follower count and delves into actionable techniques to boost engagement on social media platforms. You'll learn how to create posts that spark conversations, encourage user-generated content, and leverage the power of influencers to amplify your brand's message.

Additionally, you'll gain valuable insights into the art of storytelling and how to craft compelling narratives that resonate with your audience, thereby fostering deeper connections and increased engagement.

With the ever-evolving landscape of social media, staying up-to-date with the latest trends and best practices is crucial. This subchapter also discusses emerging trends in social media marketing, such as live video streaming, augmented reality, and chatbots. By embracing these innovations, you can stay one step ahead of your competitors and captivate your audience in new and exciting ways.

Whether you are a seasoned marketer or just starting your journey in the world of social media marketing, this subchapter provides a comprehensive guide to increasing followers and engagement. Packed with practical advice, real-world examples, and expert insights, it equips you with the tools and knowledge needed to achieve social media marketing success and drive your brand to new heights.

UTILIZING HASHTAGS AND TRENDING TOPICS

In today's digital age, hashtags and trending topics have become powerful tools for social media marketing. By understanding how to effectively use these features, marketers and advertisers can significantly boost their online presence, engage with their target audience, and drive organic traffic to their campaigns.

This subchapter aims to provide you with a comprehensive guide on leveraging hashtags and trending topics to maximize your social media marketing success.

Hashtags are not just a trendy symbol anymore; they have become an essential part of social media communication. These keywords or phrases, preceded by the pound sign (#), allow users to discover and engage with specific topics, interests, or conversations. By incorporating relevant and popular hashtags into your social media posts, you can increase your visibility and reach a wider audience. However, it is crucial to research and choose the most appropriate hashtags for your niche.

To effectively utilize hashtags, start by identifying the most popular ones within your industry or target audience. Tools like Hashtagify and RiteTag can help you discover trending hashtags and analyze their performance. Once you have a list of relevant hashtags, incorporate them strategically into your posts. However, avoid overusing hashtags, as it can make your content appear spammy and reduce engagement.

Trending topics, on the other hand, refer to the most popular and widely discussed subjects on social media platforms. These topics can range from breaking news to viral challenges or events. By staying updated on trending topics, you can tap into ongoing conversations and generate relevant content that captures the attention of your target audience. Platforms like Twitter and Facebook often feature trending topics sections, which you can monitor to identify opportunities for content creation.

To leverage trending topics effectively, ensure your content aligns with the subject matter. Craft engaging posts, articles, or videos that provide unique perspectives or valuable insights related to the trending topic. By joining the conversation, you can increase your reach and engagement, as users are more likely to interact with content that is timely and relevant.

In conclusion, hashtags and trending topics are powerful tools for social media marketers and advertisers. By utilizing these features strategically, you can expand your online reach, engage with your target audience, and drive organic traffic to your campaigns. Remember to research hashtags thoroughly, incorporate them strategically, and stay updated on trending topics to maximize your social media marketing success.

CHAPTER 4

CONTENT MARKETING ON SOCIAL MEDIA

CREATING HIGH-QUALITY AND VALUABLE CONTENT

In the world of social media marketing, content is king. The success of any marketing campaign hinges on the quality and value of the content being shared. To engage your audience, build brand awareness, and drive conversions, it is crucial to create high-quality and valuable content.

This subchapter will delve into the key strategies and principles for crafting content that resonates with your target audience.

One of the fundamental aspects of creating high-quality content is understanding your audience. By conducting thorough market research and developing buyer personas, you can gain insights into their interests, preferences, and pain points. This knowledge will enable you to tailor your content to their specific needs, ensuring it is relevant and valuable.

Furthermore, high-quality content should be informative, educational, or entertaining. It should provide value to your audience, whether it is through solving a problem, offering expert advice, or simply entertaining them. By consistently delivering valuable content, you establish your credibility and position yourself as a trusted resource within your niche.

Another crucial element in creating high-quality content is ensuring it is visually appealing. With the rise of visual-centric platforms like Instagram and Pinterest, aesthetics play a significant role in capturing your audience's attention. Utilize high-resolution images, eye-catching graphics, and visually appealing videos to enhance your content and make it more shareable.

Moreover, maintaining consistency in your content is key to building a strong brand presence. Establish a consistent tone, style, and voice across all your social media platforms to create a cohesive and recognizable brand image. Consistency also applies to the frequency and timing of your content. Regularly posting fresh and engaging content will keep your audience engaged and coming back for more.

Lastly, engage with your audience to foster a sense of community and build relationships. Respond to comments, address queries, and encourage discussions around your content. By actively participating in conversations, you demonstrate your commitment to providing value and establish a loyal and engaged following.

In conclusion, creating high-quality and valuable content is essential for anyone in the field of social media marketing. By understanding your audience, providing value, utilizing visual appeal, maintaining consistency, and engaging with your audience, you can create content that resonates, builds brand loyalty, and drives desired outcomes. Remember, quality over quantity should be your guiding principle, as it is the key to success in the ever-evolving world of social media marketing.

UNDERSTANDING DIFFERENT TYPES OF CONTENT

In today's digital world, content is king. As a marketer or advertiser, it is crucial to understand the different types of content available to effectively engage with your target audience. Social media marketing has proven to be a powerful

tool in reaching and connecting with customers, making it essential to have a comprehensive understanding of the various content types at your disposal.

1. Textual Content: This is the most basic form of content and includes articles, blog posts, captions, and social media updates. Textual content allows you to convey information, tell stories, and educate your audience. It is important to create well-written and compelling text that captures attention and encourages interaction.

2. Visual Content: Visual content includes images, infographics, videos, and GIFs. It is a highly effective way to capture the attention of your audience and convey information in an engaging manner. Visuals can be used to showcase products, demonstrate how-to guides, or simply entertain and inspire your followers.

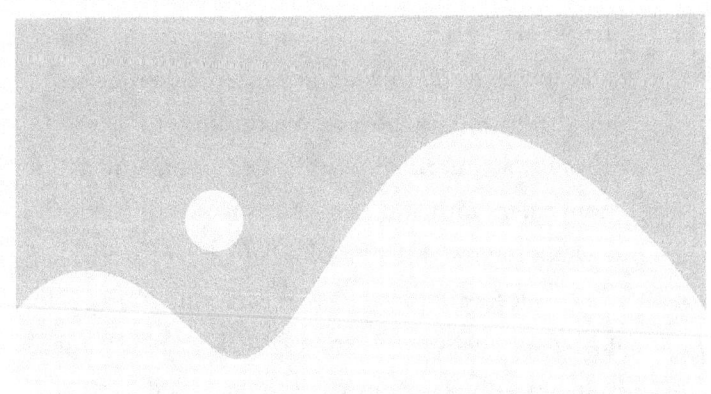

3. User-Generated Content: User- generated content (UGC) is created by your audience, such as customer reviews, testimonials, and social media posts featuring your brand. UGC is powerful because it adds authenticity and social proof to your marketing efforts. Encouraging your customers to create and share content related to your brand can significantly increase your reach and credibility.

4. Interactive Content: Interactive content encourages audience participation and engagement. It includes quizzes, polls, surveys, contests, and interactive videos. By involving your audience in the content creation process, you can create a more personalized and memorable experience, increasing brand loyalty and driving conversions.

5. Audio Content: With the rise of podcasts and audio streaming platforms, audio content has become increasingly popular. It includes podcasts, audiobooks, and voice- activated assistants. Audio content allows you to reach your audience while they are on the go and provides an opportunity to deliver valuable information and entertainment in a convenient format.

Understanding the different types of content available is essential for a successful social media marketing strategy. By leveraging a combination of textual, visual, user-generated, interactive, and audio content, you can create a diverse and engaging content mix that resonates with your target audience. Remember to tailor your content to each social media platform and continuously analyze and optimize your efforts to ensure maximum impact and success.

IMPLEMENTING CONTENT STRATEGY AND PLANNING

In the rapidly evolving world of social media marketing, effective content strategy and planning have become crucial for anyone in marketing and advertising. The success of a social media campaign heavily relies on the quality and relevance of the content being shared.

This subchapter will delve into the essential steps and best practices for implementing a robust content strategy that aligns with your social media marketing goals.

The first step in implementing a successful content strategy is to define your target audience and understand their preferences and interests. By conducting thorough market research

and audience analysis, you can gain valuable insights into the demographics, psychographics, and online behaviors of your audience.

This information will enable you to create content that resonates with them, increasing engagement and conversion rates.

Once you have a clear understanding of your target audience, you can move on to developing a content plan. This plan should outline the topics, formats, and distribution channels that will be used to reach your audience effectively. It is essential to consider the different social media platforms and their unique characteristics when determining the best distribution channels for your content.

Creating compelling and valuable content is the cornerstone of any successful social media marketing campaign. Your content should be informative, entertaining, and visually appealing to capture the attention of your audience. Incorporating storytelling techniques and leveraging user-generated content can also boost engagement and create a sense of community around your brand.

In addition to creating content, it is equally important to have a systematic approach to content scheduling and publishing. By establishing a content calendar, you can ensure a consistent and timely delivery of content across various social media platforms. This calendar should encompass key dates, events, and promotions relevant to your audience, enabling you to plan and prepare content in advance.

Analyzing the performance of your content is crucial for refining and optimizing your social media marketing efforts. Utilizing analytics tools, you can track important metrics such as reach, engagement, and conversion rates. These insights will help you identify the content types and topics that resonate most with your audience, allowing you to fine-tune your content strategy for maximum impact.

Implementing a well-defined content strategy and planning process is indispensable for anyone in marketing and advertising, particularly in the niche of social media marketing. By understanding your audience, creating compelling content, scheduling strategically, and analyzing performance, you can effectively leverage social media platforms to achieve your marketing goals and drive business success.

LEVERAGING USER-GENERATED CONTENT

In today's digital age, social media marketing has become an essential tool for businesses to connect with their target audience. The power of social media lies in its ability to facilitate user-generated content (UGC), which refers to any form of content created by users or consumers. This subchapter explores the various ways marketers can harness the potential of UGC to drive their social media marketing strategies towards success.

User-generated content serves as a valuable asset for businesses, as it not only engages their audience but also builds trust and authenticity.

Consumers are more likely to trust recommendations from fellow users rather than brand-generated content. By leveraging UGC, marketers can tap into the power of social proof and harness the influence of satisfied customers to expand their reach and attract new customers.

One effective way to leverage UGC is through contests and giveaways.

Encouraging users to create and share content related to your brand or product in exchange for a chance to win prizes is a win-win situation. It not only stimulates user engagement but also generates a buzz around your brand as users share their experiences and creations on their social media platforms.

Another strategy to leverage UGC is by featuring customer testimonials and reviews prominently on your social media channels. Sharing positive feedback from satisfied customers not only boosts brand credibility but also serves as social proof for potential customers. By encouraging customers to leave reviews and testimonials, businesses can gather an abundance of UGC that can be repurposed across various marketing channels.

Influencer marketing is another avenue where UGC plays a crucial role. Partnering with influencers to promote your brand or product can significantly enhance your social media marketing efforts. By allowing influencers to create their own content around your brand, you can tap into their creativity and authenticity to connect with their followers in a more genuine way.

Lastly, actively engaging with UGC by responding to comments, sharing user content, and incorporating user ideas and suggestions into your marketing campaigns can foster a sense of community and loyalty among your audience. By valuing and acknowledging user contributions, you can build stronger relationships and create a sense of ownership among your customers.

In conclusion, user-generated content is a powerful tool in social media marketing. By leveraging UGC, businesses can tap into the authenticity, trust, and creativity of their audience to enhance their brand image, expand their reach, and ultimately achieve success in their marketing efforts.

ANALYZING AND OPTIMIZING CONTENT PERFORMANCE

In the fast-paced world of social media marketing, it is crucial for marketers and advertisers to continually analyze and optimize their content performance. With the ever-growing number of platforms and the increasing competition for attention, understanding how your content is performing can make all the difference in achieving success.

This subchapter will dive into the key strategies and tools that can help anyone in marketing and/or advertising to effectively analyze and optimize their content performance in the realm of social media marketing.

The first step in analyzing content performance is setting measurable goals. Whether it's increasing brand awareness, driving website traffic, or generating leads, clearly defining your objectives will allow you to track and measure the success of your efforts. By using analytics tools provided by social media platforms, you can gain valuable insights into the performance of your content, such as engagement metrics, reach, and conversions.

Next, it is important to identify and understand your target audience. Conducting thorough market research and utilizing audience analysis tools will enable you to tailor your content to resonate with your specific niche. By understanding your audience's preferences, interests, and pain points, you can create content that is more likely to drive engagement and conversions.

Once you have gathered data on your content performance and audience insights, it's time to optimize your strategy. This involves refining your content creation process, distribution channels, and messaging to better align with your goals and audience preferences. A/B testing different variations of your content, experimenting with new formats, and leveraging user-generated content can help you identify what works best for your target audience.

In addition to optimizing your content, it is crucial to stay up to date with the latest trends and changes in the social media landscape. Platforms are constantly evolving, introducing new features, and updating their algorithms. Keeping a pulse on these changes will allow you to adapt your strategy accordingly and stay ahead of the competition.

In conclusion, analyzing and optimizing content performance is a fundamental aspect of social media marketing. By setting clear goals, understanding your audience, and utilizing analytics tools, you can continuously refine your strategy to achieve optimal results. Remember to stay agile and adapt to the ever- changing social media landscape to maximize your success in the niche of social media marketing.

CHAPTER 5

ADVERTISING AND PROMOTION ON SOCIAL MEDIA

INTRODUCTION TO SOCIAL MEDIA ADVERTISING

In today's digital age, social media has become an integral part of our lives. It has revolutionized the way we communicate, share information, and connect with others. With millions of users active on various social media platforms, it has become an exceptional tool for businesses to reach and engage with their target audience. This subchapter, titled "Introduction to Social Media Advertising," aims to provide anyone in marketing and/or advertising, particularly those in the niche of social media marketing, with a comprehensive understanding of the fundamentals and strategies for success in this rapidly evolving field.

The power of social media advertising lies in its ability to precisely target specific demographics and interests. Unlike traditional advertising methods, social media platforms allow

marketers to gather valuable user data, enabling them to create highly targeted campaigns.

This subchapter will explore the various social media platforms that offer advertising opportunities, such as Facebook, Instagram, Twitter, LinkedIn, and YouTube. Each platform has its unique features, user demographics, and advertising formats, and we will delve into the specifics of leveraging these platforms effectively.

Furthermore, this subchapter will provide insights into the different types of social media advertising, including display ads, sponsored content, Influencer collaborations, and more. We will discuss the advantages and disadvantages of each method, along with real-life examples to illustrate their effectiveness.

Additionally, we will highlight the importance of setting clear objectives, defining target audiences, and crafting compelling ad content that resonates with users.

Measuring success is crucial in any marketing campaign, and social media advertising is no exception. Understanding

key performance indicators (KPIs) and analytics tools is essential for evaluating the effectiveness of social media ads. We will discuss metrics such as reach, engagement, click-through rates, conversion rates, and return on investment (ROI). By analyzing these metrics, marketers can refine their strategies, optimize their campaigns, and ultimately achieve better results.

Lastly, this subchapter will explore emerging trends and best practices in social media advertising. With the constant evolution of social media platforms, it is crucial to stay updated on the latest features and techniques. We will discuss the rise of video advertising, the importance of mobile optimization, the impact of user-generated content, and the growing significance of Influencer marketing.

In conclusion, "Introduction to Social Media Advertising" aims to equip anyone in marketing and/or advertising, specifically those in the niche of social media

marketing, with the knowledge and strategies necessary for success in leveraging social media platforms for advertising purposes. By understanding the fundamentals, exploring various platforms and advertising types, measuring success, and staying ahead of emerging trends, marketers can harness the full potential of social media advertising and achieve their marketing objectives.

CHOOSING THE RIGHT AD FORMATS AND OBJECTIVES

In today's digital age, social media marketing has become an essential component of any marketing and advertising strategy. With billions of people actively engaging on various social media platforms, it provides businesses with a vast audience to connect with and promote their products or services. However, in order to effectively utilize social media marketing, it is crucial to choose the right ad formats and objectives that align with your marketing goals.

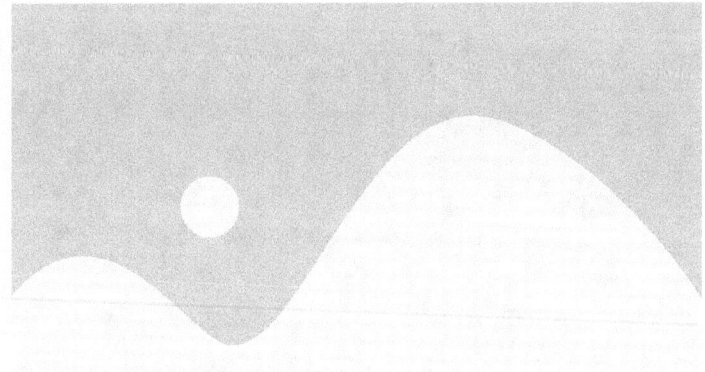

When it comes to ad formats, social media platforms offer a wide range of options to suit different marketing objectives. For instance, if your goal is to increase brand awareness, you may consider using display ads or sponsored posts that appear in users' news feeds. These formats allow you to showcase your brand and capture users' attention as they scroll through their social media accounts.

On the other hand, if your objective is to drive traffic to your website or generate leads, you might want to explore options such as video ads or carousel ads. These formats allow you to engage users with compelling visuals and a call-to-action, enticing them to click through to your website or landing page.

It is also important to consider the specific ad formats available on each social media platform. For instance, Instagram offers photo ads, video ads, and stories ads, while Facebook provides carousel ads, canvas ads, and instant

experience ads. By understanding the unique features and capabilities of each platform, you can choose the ad formats that best resonate with your target audience.

In addition to ad formats, defining clear objectives is equally important in social media marketing. Common objectives include increasing brand awareness, driving website traffic, generating leads, or boosting sales. By clearly defining your objectives, you can align your ad formats and content with your desired outcomes.

Furthermore, social media platforms provide various objective options to help you achieve your marketing goals. For example, Facebook offers objectives such as brand awareness, reach, engagement, traffic, lead generation, and conversions. By selecting the most

relevant objective, the platform will optimize your ads to maximize your chances of success.

In conclusion, choosing the right ad formats and objectives is essential for effective social media marketing. By understanding the available ad formats on different platforms and aligning them with your marketing goals, you can create engaging and impactful campaigns that resonate with your target audience. Remember to define clear objectives to

ensure your ads are optimized for success.

With the right strategy, social media marketing can be a powerful tool to grow your business and achieve marketing success.

TARGETING AND RETARGETING STRATEGIES

In the ever-evolving landscape of social media marketing, it is crucial for marketers and advertisers to understand the importance of targeting and retargeting strategies.

These strategies not only help businesses reach their desired audience effectively but also optimize their marketing efforts to achieve maximum results.

This subchapter will delve into the world of targeting and retargeting, exploring various techniques and tactics that can be employed to enhance social media marketing campaigns.

Targeting is the process of narrowing down your audience to a specific group of individuals who are most likely to be interested in your product or service. By identifying key demographic factors such as age, gender, location, and interests, marketers can create targeted content that resonates with their audience on a deeper level. This ensures that their message reaches the right

people, resulting in higher engagement rates and better conversion rates.

One powerful targeting strategy is utilizing the data collected from social media platforms. These platforms provide marketers with a vast amount of information about their users, including their preferences, behaviors, and online activities. By leveraging this data, marketers can create highly personalized content that speaks directly to their target audience.

Retargeting, on the other hand, involves reaching out to individuals who have already shown interest in your brand or products. It works by tracking users who have visited your website or engaged with your social media content and delivering targeted ads to them across various platforms. This strategy helps to keep your brand top of mind and encourages potential customers to take the desired action, such as making a purchase or signing up for a newsletter.

There are several retargeting techniques that marketers can employ. One common method is pixel-based retargeting, which involves placing a code snippet, known as a pixel, on your website. This pixel tracks visitors and allows you to deliver personalized ads to them when they browse other websites or social media platforms.

Another effective retargeting strategy is email retargeting. By collecting email addresses from website visitors or customers, marketers can send tailored email campaigns that remind recipients of their interest in the brand and encourage them to take the next step in the customer journey.

In conclusion, targeting and retargeting strategies are essential tools in the arsenal of social media marketers and advertisers. By precisely identifying and reaching out to their desired audience, businesses can optimize their marketing efforts, increase engagement, and drive conversions. By implementing the techniques discussed in this subchapter, marketers can unlock the full potential of social media marketing and achieve success in their campaigns.

BUDGETING AND BIDDING IN SOCIAL MEDIA ADVERTISING

In today's ever-evolving digital landscape, social media marketing has emerged as a powerful tool for businesses to reach and engage with their target audience. As a marketer or advertiser, understanding how to effectively allocate your budget and optimize your bidding strategies in social media advertising is crucial for achieving success in this highly competitive field.

Budgeting is the foundation of any marketing campaign, and social media advertising is no exception. When it comes to allocating your budget, it is essential to evaluate your goals, target audience, and desired outcomes. By setting clear objectives, you can determine how much you are willing to invest in each social media platform and allocate your resources accordingly.

One key aspect of budgeting is determining the right balance between paid and organic content. While organic reach on social media platforms has significantly declined over the years, it still plays a vital role in enhancing brand visibility and engagement. Allocating a portion of your budget towards content creation, community management, and building an organic following can yield long-term benefits.

However, paid advertising is where you can truly leverage the power of social media platforms. Different platforms offer various advertising options, including sponsored posts, display ads, video ads, and more. Understanding the strengths and limitations of each platform will help you optimize your budget allocation for maximum impact. For instance, Facebook's robust targeting options make it an ideal platform for reaching a specific audience, while Instagram may be more suitable for visually-driven campaigns.

Once you have allocated your budget, optimizing your bidding strategies becomes crucial. Social media platforms employ various bidding models, including cost-per-click (CPC), cost-per-impression (CPM), and cost-per-action (CPA). It is essential to analyze your campaign objectives and select the bidding model that aligns with your goals. For example, if your objective is to drive traffic to your website, CPC bidding may be more appropriate, while CPM bidding can be useful for brand awareness campaigns.

Furthermore, continuously monitoring and analyzing your campaign's performance is key to optimizing your bidding strategy. Social media platforms offer robust analytics and reporting tools that provide valuable insights into audience engagement, conversion rates, and cost per acquisition. By regularly analyzing this data, you can make informed decisions and adjust your bidding strategy to maximize your return on investment.

In conclusion, budgeting and bidding in social media advertising are critical components of any successful marketing campaign. By understanding your goals, target audience, and the strengths of each social media platform, you can effectively allocate your budget and optimize your bidding strategies for maximum impact. Continuous monitoring and analysis of your campaign's performance will enable you to make data-driven decisions and achieve success in the dynamic world of social media marketing.

TRACKING AND MEASURING AD PERFORMANCE

In the fast-paced world of social media marketing, it is crucial for marketers and advertisers to effectively track and measure the performance of their ads. By doing so, they can gain valuable insights into the success of their campaigns and make data-driven decisions to optimize their strategies. This subchapter explores the various techniques and tools available to track and measure ad performance in social media marketing, empowering anyone in marketing and/or advertising to achieve success in this dynamic field.

One of the primary ways to track and measure ad performance is through the use of analytics. Social media platforms offer robust analytics tools that provide marketers with detailed data on ad reach, engagement, conversions, and more.

By analyzing this data, marketers can determine which ads are resonating with their target audience and adjust their strategies accordingly. These analytics tools also allow marketers to track key performance indicators (KPIs) such

as click- through rates, conversion rates, and cost per acquisition, enabling them to measure the overall effectiveness of
their campaigns.

Another effective method to track ad performance is
through the use of unique tracking URLs or UTM parameters. By appending UTM parameters to the URLs of their
ads, marketers can track the traffic generated by each indi-
vidual ad. This helps them identify which ads are driving
the most traffic, conversions, and revenue, enabling them to
allocate their resources effectively.

Furthermore, conversion tracking is an essential aspect
of measuring ad performance. By setting up conversion
tracking pixels or codes on their websites, marketers can
track the actions taken by users who clicked on their ads.
This allows them to measure the number of conversions
generated by each ad, whether it be a purchase, sign-up,
or any other desired action. Armed with this information,
marketers can optimize their campaigns to drive higher
conversion rates.

In addition to platform-specific analytics and tracking
methods, there are also third-party tools and software available to track and measure ad performance across multiple
social media platforms. These tools provide marketers with
a comprehensive view of their ad performance, allowing
them to compare results across different platforms and make
informed decisions about their advertising budgets.

Tracking and measuring ad performance is an ongoing
process in social media marketing. By leveraging analytics,
unique tracking URLs, conversion tracking, and third-party

tools, marketers and advertisers can gain valuable insights into the effectiveness of their campaigns. Armed with this knowledge, they can continuously optimize their strategies, allocate their resources effectively, and achieve success in the ever-evolving world of social media marketing.

CHAPTER 6

INFLUENCER MARKETING AND PARTNERSHIPS

UNDERSTANDING INFLUENCER MARKETING

In the ever-evolving world of social media marketing, Influencer marketing has emerged as a powerful tool for brands to connect with their target audience. This sub-chapter aims to provide a comprehensive understanding of Influencer marketing and its significance in the realm of social media marketing. Whether you are a marketing professional or an advertiser, this chapter will equip you with the knowledge and strategies needed to harness the full potential of Influencer marketing.

Influencer marketing refers to the practice of leveraging individuals with a significant online following and influence to promote products or services. These individuals, known as influencers, have built a loyal and engaged audience through their expertise, authenticity, and relatability. By partnering with influencers, brands can tap into their credibility and reach to effectively reach their target market.

The first section of this subchapter delves into the importance of Influencer marketing in today's digital landscape. It explores how influencers have become the new trusted voices, replacing traditional advertising methods. With the rise of ad-blockers and the decline of traditional media consumption, Influencer marketing offers a unique opportunity for brands to cut through the noise and engage with their audience in a more authentic and impactful way.

The second section focuses on the process of identifying and selecting the right influencers for your brand. It discusses the various types of influencers, from macro-influencers with millions of followers to micro- influencers with a more niche but highly engaged audience. It also outlines key factors to consider when evaluating influencers, such as relevance, reach, engagement, and authenticity.

The third section explores the different approaches to Influencer collaborations, including sponsored content, brand partnerships, and ambassador programs. It provides insights into best practices for establishing successful Influencer- brand relationships and offers tips on negotiating contracts, setting expectations, and measuring campaign success.

Lastly, this subchapter discusses the ethical considerations and potential challenges of Influencer marketing. It emphasizes the importance of transparency and disclosure to maintain trust with the audience and comply with advertising

regulations. It also highlights the need for ongoing monitoring and evaluation to ensure the effectiveness and ROI of Influencer.

By the end of this subchapter, you will have a comprehensive understanding of Influencer marketing and the strategies needed to incorporate it into your social media marketing efforts. Whether you are a seasoned marketer or just starting out in the field, this knowledge will empower you to leverage the power of influencers to drive brand awareness, engagement, and ultimately, business success.

RESEARCHING AND IDENTIFYING RELEVANT INFLUENCERS

In the ever-evolving world of social media marketing, the power of influencers cannot be underestimated. These individuals have the ability to sway opinions, shape trends, and drive consumer behavior like never before. As a marketer or advertiser,

it is crucial to identify and collaborate with the right influencers to amplify your brand message and reach your target audience effectively.

Researching and identifying relevant influencers is a critical step in any social media marketing strategy. It involves a systematic approach to finding individuals or groups who have a significant following and whose interests align with your brand. Here's a comprehensive guide to help you navigate this process successfully.

The first step is to define your target audience and understand their preferences, interests, and online behavior. This knowledge will guide you in identifying influencers who resonate with your audience and can effectively communicate your brand message. Utilize social media analytics tools and conduct audience surveys to gather data that will inform your Influencer selection.

Next, leverage social media platforms and specialized Influencer marketing tools to conduct thorough research. Look for influencers who have a substantial following, high engagement rates, and a consistent posting frequency. Pay attention to the quality of their content and the authenticity of their interactions with followers. Look for influencers whose values align with your brand and who have a track record of promoting products or services similar to yours.

Additionally, consider the niche or industry in which you operate. Identify influencers who have expertise or a significant following within your niche. These influencers will have a deeper understanding of your target audience and will be able to establish a stronger connection with them.

When engaging with potential influencers, take the time to analyze their past collaborations and partnerships. Review their sponsored content to gauge their ability to seamlessly incorporate brand messaging without compromising authenticity. Look for influencers who have a history

Lastly, establish a strong relationship with the influencers you choose to work with. Approach them professionally, clearly communicate your expectations, and be transparent about your goals and budget. Consider offering them exclusive access to products, services, or events to incentivize their participation and maintain their enthusiasm.

Researching and identifying relevant influencers is an ongoing process. Continuously monitor their performance, track the impact of their collaborations, and adapt your strategies accordingly. By investing time and effort into this crucial step, you can harness the power of influencers to elevate your social media marketing efforts and drive tangible results.

BUILDING RELATIONSHIPS AND NEGOTIATING PARTNERSHIPS

In the fast-paced world of social media marketing, building strong relationships and negotiating partnerships are essential for success. With the ever-expanding reach of

social media platforms, it has become crucial for anyone in marketing and/or advertising to develop effective strategies to foster relationships and form partnerships that can propel their brand forward in the competitive landscape of social media marketing.

One of the key aspects of building relationships in social media marketing is understanding the importance of engagement. It is no longer enough to simply post content and hope for the best. Brands need to actively engage with their audience, respond to comments and messages, and actively participate in conversations. By doing so, brands can build trust, establish credibility, and create a loyal community of followers who are more likely to advocate for their brand.

Another vital aspect of building relationships is Influencer marketing. Collaborating with influencers who have a strong presence in a specific niche can significantly boost a brand's reach and credibility. It is essential to identify the right influencers who align with your brand's values and target audience. By developing authentic partnerships with influencers, brands can tap into their followers' trust and loyalty, leading to increased brand awareness and customer acquisition.

Negotiating partnerships is another crucial skill that anyone in social media marketing needs to master. Strategic partnerships can help brands tap into new markets, gain access to new audiences, and leverage the expertise of complementary brands.

When negotiating partnerships, it is essential to clearly define roles, expectations, and goals to ensure a mutually beneficial relationship.

By working together with partners, brands can access shared resources, cross-promote each other's content, and create innovative marketing campaigns that captivate their target audience.

Moreover, building relationships and negotiating partnerships also involves effective communication and active listening. Brands need to understand the needs and preferences of their target audience, as well as the goals and objectives of their potential partners. By actively listening and engaging in two-way conversations, brands can foster a collaborative and mutually beneficial relationship with their audience and partners.

In conclusion, building relationships and negotiating partnerships are critical skills for anyone in marketing and/or advertising,

particularly in the niche of social media marketing. By focusing on engagement, Influencer marketing, and strategic partnerships, brands can foster strong relationships, gain credibility, and expand their reach in the ever-evolving world of social media marketing.

CREATING EFFECTIVE INFLUENCER CAMPAIGNS

In today's digital age, social media marketing has become an essential component of any successful marketing and advertising strategy. With the rise of social media platforms, brands now have the opportunity to reach and engage with their target audience in a more personalized and meaningful way. One of the most powerful tools in the realm of social media marketing is Influencer campaigns.

Influencer campaigns involve partnering with individuals who have a significant following and influence in specific niches. These influencers have the ability to sway the opinions and purchasing decisions of their followers, making them valuable assets for brands looking to expand their reach. However, creating effective Influencer campaigns requires careful planning and execution. Here are some key strategies to consider:

1. Identify the Right Influencers: It's crucial to find influencers whose values, audience, and content align with your brand. Conduct thorough research to determine if an Influencer's followers match your target demographic. Look for influencers who have a genuine interest in your niche and a history of engagement with their audience.

2. Establish Clear Objectives: Before launching an Influencer campaign, define your goals. Are you looking to increase brand awareness, drive sales, or promote a specific product? Having clear objectives will help guide your campaign strategy and measure its success.

3. Authenticity is Key: Audiences are increasingly skeptical of sponsored content, so it's crucial to ensure your Influencer campaigns feel authentic. Encourage influencers to create content that reflects their personal style and voice while integrating your brand's messaging subtly.

4. Build Relationships: Successful Influencer campaigns go beyond one-o partnerships. Invest time in building relationships with influencers by engaging with their content and supporting their work. By nurturing these relationships, you can create long-term collaborations that benefit both parties.

5. Track and Measure Results: To determine the success of your Influencer campaign, establish key performance indicators (KPIs). Track metrics such as reach, engagement, website traffic, and conversions. Use these insights to optimize future campaigns and maximize your ROI.

In conclusion, Influencer campaigns are a powerful tool in the world of social media marketing. By identifying the right influencers, setting clear objectives, prioritizing authenticity, building relationships, and tracking results, you can create effective Influencer campaigns that drive real results for your brand.

Embrace the potential of Influencer marketing and leverage the power of social media to propel your marketing and advertising efforts to new heights.

MEASURING THE SUCCESS OF INFLUENCER MARKETING

In the ever-evolving landscape of social media marketing, Influencer marketing has emerged as a powerful strategy to engage with target audiences and drive brand awareness. As a marketer or advertiser in the realm of social media marketing, it is essential to measure the success of Influencer marketing campaigns to determine their impact and optimize future strategies.

One of the key metrics for measuring the success of Influencer marketing is reach. By analyzing the number of followers an Influencer has and the potential reach of their content, marketers can gauge the extent of their campaign's exposure. This metric provides valuable insights into the initial impact and visibility of the brand's message among the target audience.

Engagement is another crucial metric for evaluating the success of Influencer marketing. It goes beyond reach to assess how effectively the campaign has resonated with the audience. Monitoring likes, comments, shares, and other forms of interaction provides a deeper understanding of the level of engagement and the overall sentiment towards the brand. By analyzing engagement, marketers can identify the content that generates the most interest and tailor future campaigns accordingly.

Conversion rate is a fundamental metric that evaluates the effectiveness of Influencer marketing in driving actual business results. It measures the percentage of viewers who took the desired action, such as making a purchase, signing up for a newsletter, or downloading an app. By tracking conversion rates, marketers can determine the return on investment (ROI) of their Influencer marketing campaigns and adjust their strategies to maximize conversions.

Brand sentiment is an important metric for any social media marketing campaign, including Influencer marketing. It measures the overall perception of the brand among the target audience. By assessing sentiment through sentiment analysis tools or monitoring customer feedback and reviews, marketers can gauge how well the Influencer's content aligns with the brand's values and messaging.

Positive sentiment indicates that the campaign has successfully conveyed the desired brand image, while negative sentiment may necessitate adjustments to the Influencer selection or campaign strategy.

In conclusion, measuring the success of Influencer marketing campaigns is vital for anyone in the fields of marketing and advertising, particularly within the niche of social media marketing. By analyzing metrics such as reach, engagement, conversion rates, and brand sentiment, marketers can gain valuable insights into the effectiveness and impact of their Influencer marketing efforts. These measurements allow for optimization, enabling marketers to refine their strategies, connect with target audiences more effectively, and ultimately drive successful outcomes for their brands.

CHAPTER 7

SOCIAL MEDIA ANALYTICS AND REPORTING

IMPORTANCE OF ANALYTICS
IN SOCIAL MEDIA MARKETING

In the fast-paced world of social media marketing, staying ahead of the game is crucial. With millions of users engaging with various platforms every day, it becomes increasingly important to understand the impact and effectiveness of your marketing efforts. This is where analytics come into play. Analytics in social media marketing provide invaluable insights and data that can guide your strategies, drive better decision-making, and ultimately lead to success.

One of the main reasons why analytics is crucial in social media marketing is the ability to measure your performance. By tracking key metrics such as engagement rates, reach, impressions, and conversions, you can gain a clear understanding of how your content is resonating with your audience. This data allows you to identify what is working well and what needs improvement, enabling you to fine-tune your campaigns for maximum impact.

Moreover, analytics can help you identify and target the right audience. By analyzing demographic data, user behavior, and interests, you can create more focused and personalized content that speaks directly to your target market. This not only increases the chances of engagement but also helps in building a loyal customer base.

Additionally, analytics can uncover valuable insights about your competition. By monitoring their social media presence, tracking their engagement, and analyzing their content strategy, you can gain a competitive edge. Understanding what works for your competitors and what doesn't can help you refine your own approach and stand out from the crowd.

Furthermore, analytics can help you optimize your advertising budget. By tracking the performance of your paid campaigns, you can determine which ads are generating the highest return on investment. This data allows you to allocate your budget more effectively, ensuring that your marketing efforts are delivering the desired results.

In conclusion, analytics play a vital role in social media marketing. They provide marketers with the necessary tools and information to measure performance, target the right audience, gain a competitive edge, and optimize their advertising budgets. By leveraging analytics effectively, marketers can make data- driven decisions, refine their strategies, and achieve success in the ever- evolving world of social media marketing.

TRACKING KEY PERFORMANCE INDICATORS (KPIS)

In the fast-paced world of social media marketing, it is vital to measure and track your efforts to ensure success.

This subchapter will delve into the importance of tracking Key Performance Indicators (KPIs) and how they can help you optimize your social media marketing strategy.

For anyone in marketing and/or advertising, understanding and leveraging KPIs is essential to effectively measure the impact of your social media campaigns. KPIs are measurable data points that indicate the success or failure of your marketing efforts. They provide valuable insights into consumer behavior, campaign performance, and overall return on investment (ROI).

When it comes to social media marketing, there are several KPIs that are particularly relevant. These include reach, engagement, conversion rate, click-through rate (CTR), customer acquisition cost (CAC), and return on ad spend (ROAS), among others. Each of these metrics provides a unique perspective on the effectiveness

of your social media marketing efforts.

Reach is a KPI that measures the number of people who have seen your content. It helps gauge the size of your audience and the potential impact of your campaigns.

Engagement, on the other hand, measures how users interact with your content, such as likes, comments, and shares. It reflects the level of interest and connection your audience has

Conversion rate is a critical KPI as it tracks the percentage of visitors who take a desired action, such as making a purchase or filling out a form. CTR measures the number of clicks your ads receive divided by the number of impressions, indicating how compelling your ad is to your audience.

CAC is a financial KPI that calculates the cost of acquiring a new customer.

It helps you determine the effectiveness of your marketing budget and identify opportunities for improvement. ROAS, on the other hand, is a metric that measures the revenue generated from your advertising spend.

By regularly tracking these KPIs, you can identify trends, make data-driven decisions, and optimize your social media marketing strategy. It allows you to understand what works and what doesn't, helping you allocate resources effectively and achieve maximum ROI.

In conclusion, tracking Key Performance Indicators (KPIs) is vital for anyone in marketing and advertising, especially in the niche of social media marketing. By measuring and analyzing metrics such as reach, engagement, conversion rate, CTR, CAC, and ROAS, you can gain valuable insights into the success of your campaigns. These KPIs enable you to make data-driven decisions, optimize your strategies, and ultimately achieve success in your social media marketing efforts.

ANALYZING REACH, ENGAGEMENT, AND CONVERSION

In the fast-paced world of social media marketing, understanding and effectively analyzing your reach, engagement, and conversion metrics are crucial for achieving success. In this subchapter, we will delve into the importance of these metrics and how they can be leveraged to optimize your social media marketing strategies.

Reach refers to the number of unique individuals who have been exposed to your social media content. It is a fundamental metric that helps gauge the overall visibility of your brand, campaign, or product. By analyzing reach, you can assess the effectiveness of your social media efforts in terms of generating awareness and expanding your online presence. Understanding your reach enables you to identify potential gaps and opportunities for growth.

Engagement, on the other hand, measures the level of interaction and involvement your audience has with your content. It includes metrics such as likes, comments, shares, and clicks. By analyzing engagement, you gain valuable insights into the type of content that resonates with your audience, allowing you to optimize your future posts. Engaging content not only helps build a loyal community but also increases the likelihood of your brand being shared, thereby amplifying your reach and visibility.

Conversion, the ultimate goal of any marketing campaign, measures the number of users who take a desired action after engaging with your social media content. This action could be signing up for a newsletter, making a purchase, or downloading a resource. Analyzing conversion metrics helps you determine the effectiveness of your social media marketing efforts in driving real, tangible results. By understanding the conversion rate, you can identify areas for

improvement and optimize your campaigns to increase your return on investment.

To effectively analyze reach, engagement, and conversion, you need to leverage social media analytics tools. These tools provide in-depth insights into your audience demographics, behavior, and preferences. By leveraging this data, you can tailor your content to cater to the specific needs and interests of your target audience, thereby enhancing engagement and driving conversions.

In conclusion, analyzing reach, engagement, and conversion metrics is essential for anyone in marketing and/or advertising, particularly in the niche of social media marketing. By understanding and leveraging these metrics, you can optimize your social media strategies, increase brand visibility, and drive tangible results. So, dive into the world of analytics, unlock the power of data, and take your social media marketing efforts to the next level.

TOOLS AND PLATFORMS FOR SOCIAL MEDIA ANALYTICS

In today's digital age, social media has become an integral part of marketing and advertising strategies. With billions of active users across various platforms, it has become crucial for businesses to harness the power of social media to connect with their target audience and drive business growth. However, to truly succeed in social media marketing, it is essential to understand the impact of your efforts and measure the effectiveness of your campaigns. This is where tools and platforms for social media analytics come into play.

Social media analytics tools provide marketers with valuable insights and data that can help them make informed decisions, optimize their strategies, and achieve better results. These tools offer a range of features, including tracking engagement, monitoring brand mentions, analyzing competitor performance, and measuring the impact of social media campaigns.

One of the most popular social media analytics tools is Google Analytics. It allows marketers to track website traffic generated from social media, identify the most effective social platforms, and measure conversions. It also provides in-depth data on user behavior, allowing marketers to understand how their audience interacts with their content.

Another powerful tool is Hootsuite, which allows marketers to manage multiple social media accounts from a single dashboard. Hootsuite also provides analytics reports that offer insights on audience demographics, engagement rates, and top- performing content. This data can be used to refine social media strategies and create more targeted campaigns.

For those looking for a comprehensive social media analytics platform, Sprout Social is a popular choice. It offers features like social media scheduling, monitoring, and reporting. Sprout Social's analytics capabilities provide detailed data on engagement, audience growth, and sentiment analysis, enabling marketers to understand their audience's preferences and sentiments towards their brand.

Additionally, Facebook Insights, Twitter Analytics, and Instagram Insights are native analytics tools offered by these respective platforms. These tools provide valuable data on audience demographics, post reach, engagement rates, and follower growth. Marketers can use this information to optimize their content, identify trends, and engage more effectively with their audience.

In conclusion, tools and platforms for social media analytics play a crucial role in the success of social media marketing strategies. By leveraging these tools, marketers can gain valuable insights into their audience, measure the effectiveness of their campaigns, and make data-driven decisions. Whether you are a novice or an experienced marketer in the field of social media marketing, utilizing these tools and platforms can significantly enhance your marketing efforts and drive business success.

CREATING COMPREHENSIVE REPORTS AND INSIGHTS

In the ever-evolving world of social media marketing, it is crucial for marketers and advertisers to stay on top of the latest trends and strategies. One of the most effective ways to achieve success in this field is by creating comprehensive reports and gaining valuable insights from them. This sub-chapter will delve into the importance of generating detailed reports and how they can contribute to the success of your social media marketing campaigns.

Reports serve as a valuable tool for marketers and advertisers in assessing the performance of their social media marketing efforts. By collecting and analyzing data from various platforms, such as Facebook, Instagram, Twitter, and LinkedIn, you can gain a deeper understanding of your target audience's behaviors, preferences, and engagement levels. This information can then be used to make informed decisions and optimize future marketing campaigns.

To create comprehensive reports, it is essential to identify key performance indicators (KPIs) that align with your marketing objectives. These could include metrics such as reach, engagement, click-through rates, conversions, and return on investment (ROI). By tracking these KPIs over time, you can measure the effectiveness of your social media marketing strategies and make necessary adjustments to maximize your results.

In addition to collecting quantitative data, qualitative insights are equally important. This can be achieved through monitoring social media conversations, analyzing customer feedback, and conducting surveys or interviews. These qualitative insights provide a deeper understanding of your audience's sentiment, preferences, and pain points, allowing you to tailor your marketing messages and content accordingly.

Once you have gathered and analyzed the data, the next crucial step is to present your findings in a clear and concise manner. Visualizing data through charts, graphs, and infographics can help convey complex information in an easily digestible format. Use these visual aids to highlight trends, patterns, and correlations, making it easier for stakeholders to comprehend the insights and take appropriate actions.

Creating comprehensive reports and gaining valuable insights is an ongoing process. Regularly monitoring and analyzing your social media marketing efforts will enable you to identify opportunities for improvement, optimize your campaigns, and stay ahead of the competition.

In conclusion, generating comprehensive reports and gaining valuable insights are vital components of successful social media marketing strategies. By harnessing the power of data, marketers and advertisers can make informed decisions, optimize their campaigns, and ultimately achieve their marketing objectives. Stay tuned for the next chapter, where we will dive deeper into the strategies for leveraging social media platforms to maximize your marketing efforts.

CHAPTER 8

SOCIAL MEDIA CRISIS MANAGEMENT

IDENTIFYING AND RESPONDING TO POTENTIAL CRISES

In the fast-paced world of social media marketing, one cannot overlook the potential for crises to arise. With the power of social media platforms to amplify messages and spread information quickly, it is crucial for anyone in marketing and advertising, especially those in the niche of social media marketing, to be prepared to identify and respond to potential crises effectively.

The first step in crisis management is to be vigilant and proactive in identifying potential crises before they escalate. Regularly monitoring social media channels, news outlets, and industry trends can help marketers stay ahead of any emerging issues.

By paying attention to customer feedback, industry conversations, and competitor activities, marketers can detect any signs of a potential crisis brewing.

Once a potential crisis is identified, it is essential to respond promptly and transparently. Ignoring or downplaying the issue can lead to a rapid escalation and irreparable damage to a brand's reputation.

Instead, marketers should acknowledge the situation, take responsibility if necessary, and provide updates and solutions in a timely manner.

In order to effectively respond to a crisis, having a well-thought-out crisis management plan in place is crucial. This plan should outline the key steps to be taken, designate roles and responsibilities, and specify communication channels to be used. By having a pre-established crisis management plan, marketers can ensure a coordinated and consistent response, minimizing confusion and enabling quick decision-making.

Furthermore, it is important to remember that crises can take many forms in the realm of social media marketing. These may include negative reviews, customer complaints, data breaches, product recalls, or even public relations disasters.

Each crisis requires a tailored response, and it is essential to remain calm, empathetic, and focused on finding a resolution.

Additionally, leveraging social media to communicate during a crisis can be both advantageous and challenging. On one hand, social media allows for immediate and widespread communication with the target audience. On the other hand, it can also be a breeding ground for misinformation and negativity. Marketers must strike a balance between being responsive and cautious, ensuring that their messages are accurate, empathetic, and address the concerns of their audience.

In conclusion, identifying and responding to potential crises is a crucial aspect of social media marketing. By staying vigilant, having a well-prepared crisis management plan, and effectively leveraging social media, marketers can navigate through crises and protect their brand's reputation. Being proactive, transparent, and responsive will not only help mitigate the negative impact of a crisis but can also turn it into an opportunity to showcase the brand's commitment to customer satisfaction and problem-solving.

DEVELOPING A CRISIS MANAGEMENT PLAN

In the fast-paced world of social media marketing, crises can strike at any moment, causing significant damage to a brand's reputation.

That's why it is crucial for anyone in marketing and/or advertising, especially those in the niche of social media marketing, to develop a comprehensive crisis management plan. This subchapter will guide you through the steps of creating an effective plan to navigate through turbulent times and protect your brand's image.

The first step in developing a crisis management plan is to identify potential crises that could arise in the realm of social media marketing.

These can include negative customer feedback, viral controversies, data breaches, or even social media platform outages. By understanding the unique challenges that social media presents, you can proactively craft strategies to minimize the impact of these situations.

Once potential crises are identified, it's essential to establish a crisis response team. This team should consist of key individuals from various departments, including marketing, public relations, legal, and customer service.

Collaborating with cross-functional teams ensures a comprehensive approach to crisis management, allowing for swift and efficient decision-making.

Next, your crisis management plan should outline clear protocols for monitoring social media platforms. Utilize social listening tools to track brand mentions, sentiment analysis, and any emerging trends or issues. By staying vigilant, you can detect potential crises early on and respond proactively.

Preparation is key when it comes to managing crises. Develop an escalation protocol that outlines the chain of command and responsibilities for each team member. This ensures a streamlined response and prevents confusion during high-pressure situations.

Furthermore, your crisis management plan should include pre-approved messaging templates for different scenarios. These templates should be adaptable to t the

adjustments to address any shortcomings.

In conclusion, developing a crisis management plan is crucial for anyone in marketing and/or advertising, especially those in the niche of social media marketing. By identifying potential crises, establishing a crisis response team, monitoring social media platforms, preparing a response protocol, and regularly reviewing and updating your plan, you can effectively navigate through crises and protect your brand's reputation in the ever- changing world of social media.

unique circumstances of each crisis while maintaining a consistent brand voice. Train your team on using these templates effectively, ensuring a timely and unified response across all

Finally, regularly review and update your crisis management plan. Social media is constantly evolving, and new challenges may arise. By conducting regular drills and simulations, you can test the effectiveness of your plan and make necessary

HANDLING NEGATIVE FEEDBACK AND TROLLS

In the ever-evolving world of social media marketing, it is essential to understand that not all feedback will be positive. Negative feedback and trolls

can often feel like a setback, but when handled correctly, they can actually be an opportunity for growth and improvement. This subchapter will provide you with valuable insights and strategies to effectively handle negative feedback and trolls in your social media marketing campaigns.

First and foremost, it is important to remember that negative feedback is not a personal attack. It is simply an expression of someone's opinion or experience. Rather than responding defensively, take a step back and assess the feedback objectively. Is there any truth or validity to the criticism? If yes, acknowledge it and respond with empathy and a commitment to address the issue. This shows your audience that you value their feedback and are willing to make improvements.

However, it is crucial to distinguish between genuine feedback and trolls. Trolls are individuals who intentionally provoke and harass others online. They may leave offensive

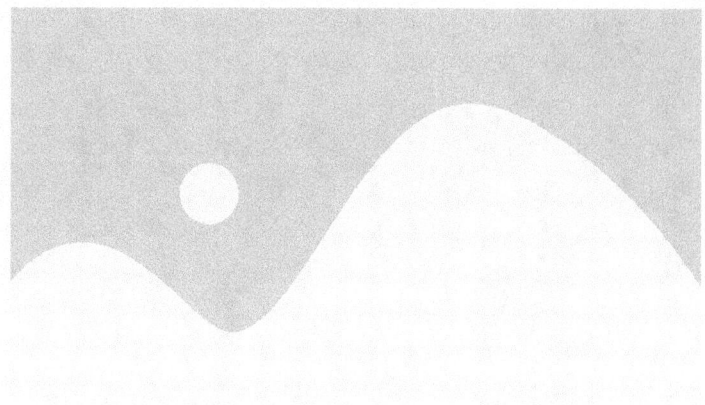

comments or engage in disruptive behavior. When dealing with trolls, it is best not to engage directly. Responding to their negativity will only fuel their re. Instead, focus on creating a positive and supportive online community. Encourage your followers to report any abusive or inappropriate comments, and promptly remove them from your page.

Another effective strategy for handling negative feedback and trolls is to take the conversation online. If someone has a legitimate concern or complaint, invite them to send a direct message or email to address the issue privately. This not only shows that you are willing to resolve their problem but also prevents a public confrontation that could potentially damage your brand's reputation.

Lastly, use negative feedback as an opportunity to learn and grow. Analyze the feedback, identify patterns or recurring issues, and make the necessary adjustments to your

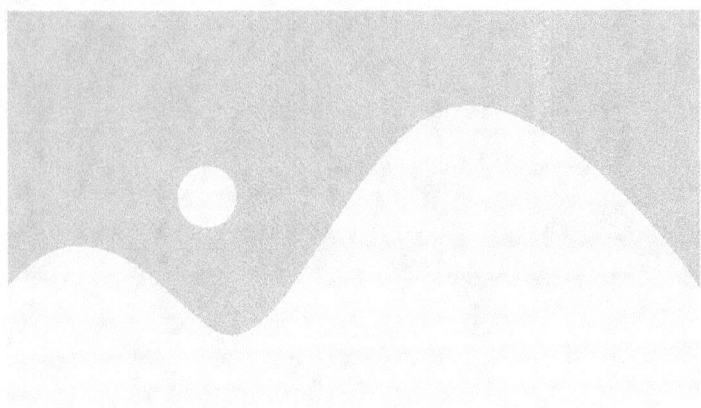

social media marketing strategy. Turn negative experiences into positive outcomes by demonstrating your ability to listen, adapt, and continuously improve.

In conclusion, handling negative feedback and trolls is an inevitable part of social media marketing. By responding with empathy, distinguishing genuine feedback from trolls, taking conversations online, and using feedback as a learning opportunity, you can turn these challenges into opportunities for growth and success. Remember, it is through adversity that we truly learn and improve.

REBUILDING REPUTATION AND TRUST

In the fast-paced world of social media marketing, reputation and trust are invaluable assets for any business or brand. In this subchapter, we will explore effective strategies for rebuilding reputation and trust, ensuring long-term success in the realm of social media marketing.

The digital landscape has given rise to unprecedented opportunities for businesses to connect with their audience, but it has also brought challenges. Negative reviews, customer complaints, and public backlash can quickly tarnish a brand's reputation. However, with the right approach, it is possible to rebuild and even enhance trust among consumers.

First and foremost, it is essential to address any negative feedback or complaints promptly and sincerely. In the age of social media, ignoring or dismissing customer concerns can be detrimental to a brand's image. By actively listening and responding empathetically, businesses can demonstrate their commitment to customer satisfaction and show that they value their audience's opinions.

Transparency is another key aspect of rebuilding reputation and trust. Being open and honest about any past mistakes or shortcomings can go a long way in rebuilding trust. Admitting to errors and outlining steps taken to rectify them will show consumers that the brand takes responsibility for its actions and is actively working towards improvement.

Collaborating with influencers and thought leaders in the industry can also help rebuild reputation and trust. Partnering with respected individuals who align with the brand's values can lend credibility and enhance the brand's image. By associating with trusted influencers, businesses can tap into their loyal following and expand their reach to a wider audience.

Furthermore, investing in social proof is crucial for rebuilding reputation and trust. Encouraging satisfied customers to leave positive reviews and testimonials can counterbalance any negative feedback. Utilizing social proof tools, such as displaying customer ratings and testimonials on the brand's website or social media profiles, can instill confidence in potential customers and help rebuild trust.

Lastly, consistency is key. Consistently delivering on promises, providing high- quality products or services, and maintaining open lines of communication will help rebuild reputation and gain the trust of consumers over time. Building a solid foundation of trust requires ongoing effort and commitment, but the long- term benefits are well worth it.

In conclusion, rebuilding reputation and trust in the ever-evolving landscape of social media marketing is a crucial aspect for any business or brand. By promptly addressing customer concerns, being transparent, collaborating with influencers, showcasing social proof, and maintaining consistency, businesses can rebuild their reputation and trust, ultimately leading to long-term success in the realm of social media marketing.

LEARNING FROM CRISIS SITUATIONS

In the fast-paced world of social media marketing, crisis situations can arise unexpectedly, causing chaos and potentially damaging a brand's reputation. However, these crises can also present unique opportunities for growth and learning. This subchapter aims to explore the valuable lessons that can be derived from crisis situations in the realm of social media marketing.

1. The importance of preparedness: Crisis situations often catch brands o guard, highlighting the significance of being prepared for any eventuality. By having a crisis management plan in place, marketers can effectively respond to issues, mitigate damage, and regain control swiftly. This subchapter will delve into the key components of an effective crisis management plan, including monitoring tools, escalation protocols, and response strategies.

2. Listening to your audience: Crisis situations often stem from a breakdown in communication or a failure to address customer concerns. By actively listening to your audience on social media platforms, marketers can identify potential issues before they escalate into full-blown crises. This subchapter will explore the various tools and techniques available for

monitoring social media conversations and sentiment analysis, empowering marketers to proactively address customer grievances.

3. Transparency and authenticity: In times of crisis, maintaining transparency and authenticity is crucial to preserving a brand's reputation. This subchapter will emphasize the importance of being honest with your audience, acknowledging mistakes, and providing timely updates. By fostering open communication channels and demonstrating genuine concern, marketers can rebuild trust and strengthen their brand in the long run.

4. Turning crisis into opportunity: While crisis situations can be challenging, they also present opportunities for growth and innovation. By carefully analyzing the root causes of a crisis, marketers can identify areas for improvement and implement necessary changes to prevent similar issues in the future. This subchapter will provide real-life examples of brands that successfully turned crisis situations into opportunities, showcasing how resilience and adaptability can lead to positive outcomes.

5. Learning from others: Finally, this subchapter will highlight the importance of learning from the experiences of other brands that have faced and overcome crisis situations in the social media marketing landscape. By studying case studies and best practices, marketers can gain valuable insights and

apply them to their own strategies, minimizing the likelihood of encountering similar issues.

6. In conclusion, crisis situations in social media marketing can be challenging, but they also offer valuable lessons that can enhance a brand's over-all approach. By being prepared, listening to their audience, maintaining transparency, and learning from past experiences, marketers can turn crises into opportunities for growth and success.

CHAPTER 9

FUTURE TRENDS AND INNOVATIONS IN SOCIAL MEDIA MARKETING

EMERGING SOCIAL MEDIA PLATFORMS AND FEATURES

In the fast-paced world of social media marketing, it is crucial for professionals in the field to stay updated with the latest platforms and features. The digital landscape is constantly evolving, and new social media platforms and features are continually emerging, offering marketers exciting opportunities to reach their target audience in innovative ways. This subchapter of "The Ultimate Guide to Social Media Marketing: Strategies for Success" aims to provide a comprehensive overview of the most promising emerging social media platforms and features, catering to anyone in marketing and/or advertising, particularly those focused on social media marketing.

1. TikTok: With its explosive growth and massive user base, TikTok has grabbed the attention of marketers worldwide. This video-sharing platform allows brands to create engaging content and leverage popular trends to reach a younger demographic. We will explore strategies to maximize brand exposure and engagement on TikTok.

2. Clubhouse: Audio-based social networking has gained momentum with the rise of Clubhouse. This invite- only platform enables marketers to host live conversations, panel discussions, and Q&A sessions, fostering genuine interactions with

users. We will delve into ways to utilize Clubhouse to build brand authority and engage with a highly targeted audience.

3. Instagram Reels: Capitalizing on the success of TikTok, Instagram launched Reels, a short-form video feature. We will discuss how to create compelling Reels content, optimize visibility, and leverage its integration with Instagram's existing tools and features to enhance brand awareness.

4. Snapchat Spotlight: As Snapchat's answer to TikTok, Spotlight focuses on user-generated short videos. We will explore how marketers can tap into this platform to showcase their

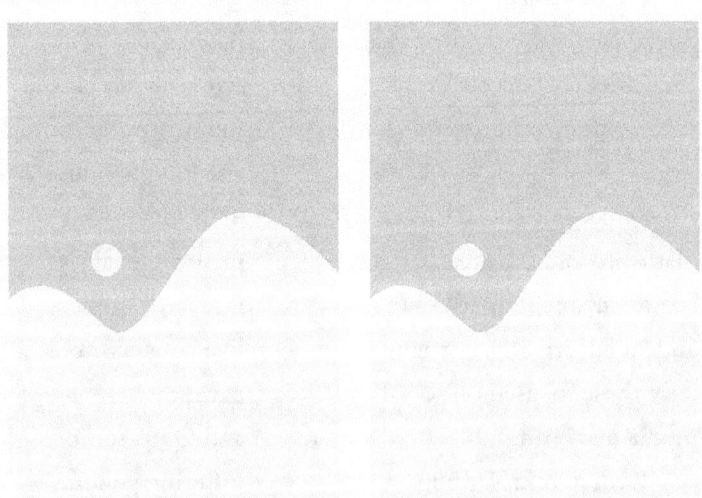

brand's creativity and connect with a younger, highly engaged audience.

5. Augmented Reality (AR): The integration of AR in social media platforms is revolutionizing the way brands engage with consumers. We will explore how AR features, such as filters and virtual try-on experiences, can enhance brand storytelling and drive conversions.

Throughout this subchapter, we will provide practical tips, case studies, and best practices to help marketers navigate these emerging platforms and features successfully. By staying ahead of the curve and embracing the opportunities presented by these new social media platforms, marketers can expand their reach, engage with their target audience, and ultimately drive business growth.

Whether you are a seasoned marketer or just starting in the field, this subchapter will equip you with the knowledge and insights necessary to leverage the power of emerging social media platforms and features to enhance your social media marketing efforts. Stay tuned as we dive into the exciting world of these emerging platforms and discover how they can elevate your marketing strategies.

ARTIFICIAL INTELLIGENCE AND CHATBOTS IN MARKETING

In today's digital age, the field of marketing is constantly evolving. The rise of social media marketing has revolutionized the way businesses connect with their target audience. And now, with the advent of artificial intelligence

(AI) and chatbots, marketers have a powerful new tool at their disposal.

Artificial intelligence refers to the simulation of human intelligence in machines that are programmed to think and learn like humans. Chatbots, on the other hand, are computer programs designed to mimic human conversation and interact with users. When combined, AI and chatbots have the potential to greatly enhance the marketing strategies of businesses across various industries.

One of the key advantages of using AI and chatbots in social media marketing is their ability to provide personalized and real-time customer support. Chatbots can be programmed to answer frequently asked questions, provide product recommendations, and even assist in completing

purchases. This level of instant support not only improves customer satisfaction but also saves time and resources for businesses.

Furthermore, AI-powered chatbots have the potential to analyze vast amounts of data and extract valuable insights. By tracking user interactions and behavior patterns on social media platforms, marketers can gain a deeper understanding of their target audience. This data can then be used to create more targeted and effective marketing campaigns, tailored to specific demographics and preferences.

In addition to customer support and data analysis, AI and chatbots can also be utilized for lead generation and conversion. By integrating chatbots into social media platforms, businesses can engage with potential customers in a more personalized manner. Chatbots can initiate conversations, gather contact information, and even guide users through the sales funnel, ultimately increasing conversion rates.

However, it is important to note that while AI and chatbots offer numerous benefits, they should not replace human interaction entirely. A balance between automation and personalization is crucial in maintaining a positive customer experience.

In conclusion, the integration of artificial intelligence and chatbots into social media marketing presents exciting opportunities for businesses. By harnessing the power of AI, marketers can provide personalized customer support, gain valuable insights, and improve lead generation and conversion rates. As technology continues to advance, it is essential for anyone in marketing and/or advertising, especially those in the niche of social media marketing, to stay updated and embrace the potential of AI and chatbots in their strategies.

VIDEO MARKETING AND LIVE STREAMING

Video Marketing and Live Streaming: Boosting Engagement and Reaching New Heights

In today's fast-paced digital world, where attention spans are shrinking and competition for eyeballs is fierce, video marketing has emerged as a powerful tool for marketers and advertisers alike. With its ability to captivate and engage audiences, video has become a must-have component of any successful social media marketing strategy.

The Rise of Video Marketing: Video content has witnessed an explosive growth and popularity on social media platforms in recent years. From short, snappy videos on TikTok to longer, informative videos on YouTube, people are consuming video content like never before. This surge in demand presents a golden opportunity for marketers to connect with their target audience on a deeper level and drive meaningful engagement.

Why Video Works: Videos have the unique ability to convey emotions, tell stories, and deliver messages in a dynamic and engaging manner. By leveraging the power of visuals, sound, and motion, marketers can create memorable experiences that resonate with their audience. Whether it's a product demonstration, a behind-the-scenes look at your brand, or a customer testimonial, video

content can evoke emotions, build trust, and ultimately drive conversions.

Harnessing the Power of Live Streaming: Live streaming takes video marketing to a whole new level by enabling real-time interactions with your audience. Platforms like Facebook Live, Instagram Live, and YouTube Live allow brands to connect with their followers in an authentic and unscripted way. Whether it's hosting Q&A sessions, conducting interviews, or showcasing live events, live streaming offers a unique opportunity to engage with your audience in real-time and build a sense of community around your brand.

Tips for Successful Video Marketing and Live Streaming:

1. Know your audience: Understand your target audience's preferences, interests, and pain points to create video content that resonates with them.

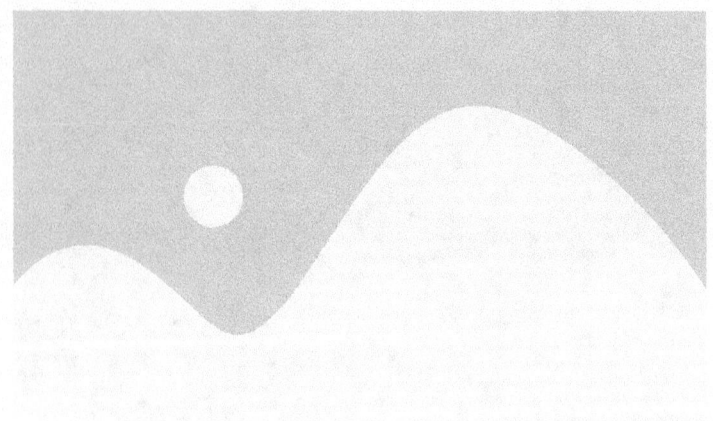

2. Plan your content: Develop a content strategy that aligns with your marketing goals and outlines the type of videos you'll create, the platforms you'll target, and the frequency of your video uploads.

3. Keep it concise: Attention spans are limited, so make sure your videos are concise, engaging, and to the point.

4. Optimize for mobile: With the majority of social media users accessing platforms through mobile devices, ensure your videos are optimized for mobile viewing.

5. Promote, promote, promote: Don't just create videos; actively promote and distribute them across your social media channels to maximize reach and engagement.

In conclusion, video marketing and live streaming are powerful tools for social media marketing success. By harnessing the emotive power of video, marketers can

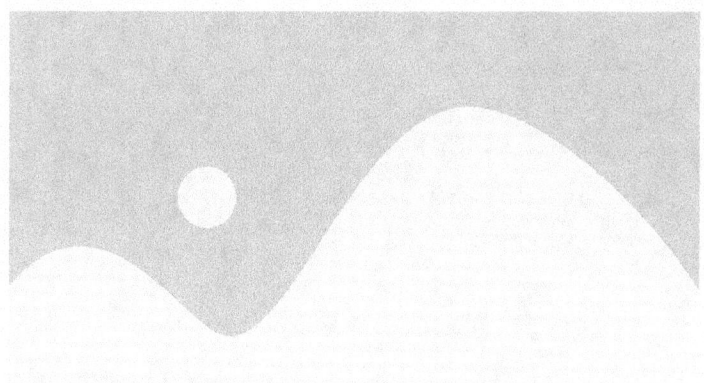

captivate their audience, build brand awareness, and drive conversions. So, whether you're a seasoned marketer or just starting out, it's time to embrace the world of video marketing and live streaming to take your social media strategy to new heights.

VIRTUAL REALITY (VR) AND AUGMENTED REALITY (AR)

Virtual Reality (VR) and Augmented Reality (AR) have emerged as game-changers in the world of social media marketing. These technologies have the power to revolutionize the way brands engage with their audience and create immersive experiences like never before. In this subchapter, we will explore the potential of VR and AR and how marketers can leverage them to drive success in the ever- evolving landscape of social media marketing.

Virtual Reality (VR) allows users to step into a computer-generated world, completely immersing themselves in a simulated environment. This technology opens up endless

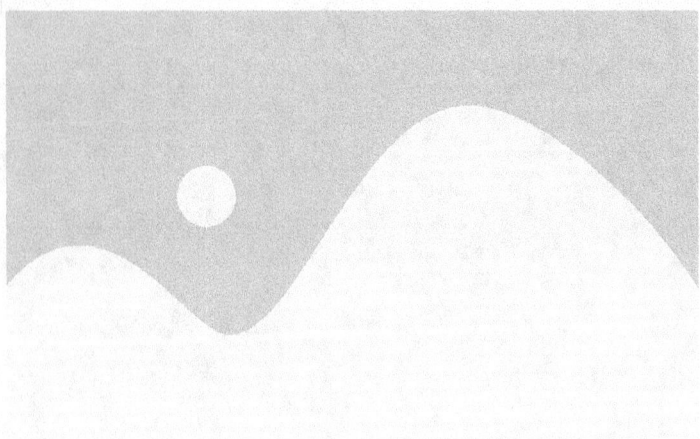

possibilities for marketers to create unique and memorable brand experiences. Imagine a fashion brand using VR to showcase their latest collection, allowing users to virtually try on the clothes and envision themselves in different settings. Such an experience not only enhances customer engagement but also increases the likelihood of conversion.

Augmented Reality (AR), on the other hand, overlays digital content onto the real world, enhancing the user's perception of reality. With AR, marketers can bridge the gap between the physical and digital worlds, offering consumers a seamless and interactive experience. For instance, a furniture retailer can use AR to enable customers to visualize how a particular piece of furniture would look in their own homes before making a purchase. This not only adds value to the customer's decision-making process but also eliminates the need for physical showrooms.

Both VR and AR have gained significant traction on social media platforms. Facebook's acquisition of Oculus

Rift for VR and the introduction of Snapchat's AR filters are just a few examples of how these technologies have seeped into the mainstream social media landscape. Marketers can leverage these platforms to reach a wider audience and create engaging content that stands out in a crowded digital space.

To successfully integrate VR and AR into social media marketing strategies, marketers need to understand their target audience and their preferences. It is essential to create experiences that are not only immersive but also align with the brand's values and resonate with the target market. Additionally, brands need to ensure that their VR and AR experiences are accessible across different devices and platforms to maximize reach and engagement

In conclusion, VR and AR have the potential to reshape the social media marketing landscape. By incorporating these technologies into their strategies, marketers can create unparalleled experiences that captivate their audience and drive business results. As social media platforms continue to evolve, embracing VR and AR will be instrumental in staying ahead of the curve and reaching new heights in social media marketing.

THE FUTURE OF SOCIAL MEDIA MARKETING

In recent years, social media marketing has become an integral part of any successful marketing and advertising strategy. With billions of people around the world using platforms such as Facebook, Instagram, Twitter, and LinkedIn, brands have recognized the immense potential of reaching and engaging with their target audience through these channels. However, as technology continues to evolve and consumer behavior shifts, it is crucial for marketers to stay ahead of the curve and understand the future trends and advancements that will shape the landscape of social media marketing.

One key aspect that will drive the future of social media marketing is the rise of artificial intelligence (AI) and machine learning. These technologies have the potential to revolutionize how marketers analyze data, automate processes, and personalize user experiences. With AI-powered algorithms, brands can gain deeper insights into consumer behavior, allowing them to create more targeted and relevant content. Additionally, chatbots and virtual assistants powered by AI will enhance customer service and provide instant responses, improving overall user satisfaction.

Another trend that will shape the future of social media marketing is the increasing importance of video content. As internet speeds continue to improve and mobile devices become more prevalent, video has become the preferred format for consuming information and entertainment. Platforms like YouTube, TikTok, and Instagram Reels have already gained massive popularity, and brands that incorporate video content into their social media strategies will be better positioned to engage their audience and drive conversions.

Furthermore, the future of social media marketing will be characterized by the growing significance of Influencer marketing. Influencers have become trusted voices in various niches, and their recommendations and endorsements hold a significant amount of sway over their followers. Collaborating with influencers allows brands to tap into their dedicated fan base and leverage their credibility to gain exposure and build brand loyalty.

Lastly, as privacy concerns continue to dominate the digital landscape, marketers will need to adapt to new regulations and consumer expectations. Stricter data protection laws, such as the General Data Protection Regulation (GDPR), and increased user awareness about data privacy will require marketers to be more transparent and ethical in their data collection and targeting practices. Building trust and fostering genuine connections with consumers will be essential for brands to succeed in the future of social media marketing.

In conclusion, the future of social media marketing holds immense opportunities for marketers and advertisers. Embracing AI and machine learning, leveraging video content, collaborating with influencers, and prioritizing privacy and transparency will be key to staying ahead in this ever-evolving landscape. By understanding these future trends and adapting their strategies accordingly, marketers can ensure their social media efforts remain effective and impactful in driving brand awareness, engagement, and ultimately, business success.

CHAPTER 10

CONCLUSION AND FINAL THOUGHTS

RECAP OF KEY STRATEGIES AND TECHNIQUES

In the rapidly evolving world of social media marketing, staying ahead of the game is essential for anyone in marketing and/or advertising. This subchapter serves as a valuable recap of the key strategies and techniques discussed throughout "The Ultimate Guide to Social Media Marketing: Strategies for Success." Whether you are a seasoned marketer or just starting out, these insights will help you navigate the ever-changing landscape of social media marketing.

One of the fundamental strategies emphasized in this book is the importance of defining clear goals and objectives for your social media marketing campaigns. By aligning your efforts with specific outcomes, such as increasing brand awareness, driving website traffic, or boosting sales, you can create more targeted and effective marketing strategies.

Another essential technique highlighted in this guide is the art of crafting compelling content. Social media platforms thrive on engaging and shareable content, and mastering the art of creating content that resonates with your target audience is crucial. From eye-catching visuals to attention-grabbing headlines, this book provides

practical tips and techniques to help you create content that stands out in a crowded digital landscape.

Furthermore, the subchapter delves into the power of Influencer marketing. Leveraging the reach and influence of social media influencers can yield impressive results for your marketing efforts. By identifying relevant influencers within your niche and building meaningful partnerships, you can tap into their engaged audiences and amplify your brand's

Additionally, the guide emphasizes the significance of data-driven decision- making. Social media platforms offer a wealth of analytics and insights that can inform your marketing strategies. By leveraging these metrics, you can gain a deeper understanding of your audience's preferences,

behavior, and engagement levels, allowing you to refine and optimize your campaigns for maximum impact.

Lastly, the subchapter highlights the importance of staying informed and adapting to the ever-changing social media landscape. Social media platforms regularly introduce new features, algorithms, and trends, and it is essential to stay updated to remain competitive. By continuously learning and experimenting with emerging strategies and techniques,

you can stay ahead of the curve and maintain a strong presence in the dynamic world of social media marketing.

In conclusion, this subchapter serves as a comprehensive recap of the key strategies and techniques discussed in "The Ultimate Guide to Social Media Marketing: Strategies for Success." Whether you are a marketing professional or an advertiser, these insights will equip you with the necessary tools to succeed in the niche of social media marketing. By implementing these strategies and staying adaptable, you can build a strong online presence, engage your target audience, and drive impactful results for your brand.

IMPLEMENTING AND ITERATING
SOCIAL MEDIA MARKETING PLANS

In today's digital age, social media marketing has become an integral part of any successful marketing and advertising strategy. With millions of users engaging on various social media platforms, it has become imperative for businesses to establish a strong presence and leverage the power of social media to reach their target audience effectively.

This subchapter delves into the key aspects of implementing and iterating social media marketing plans. Whether you are a seasoned marketer or someone new to the field, this chapter will guide you through the necessary steps to create and execute a successful social media marketing strategy.

To begin, we will discuss the importance of setting clear objectives and goals for your social media marketing efforts. Defining your objectives will help you stay focused and measure the success of your campaigns. Whether it is increasing brand awareness, driving website traffic, or generating leads, having a clear vision will guide your actions and ensure that your efforts align with your overall marketing goals.

Next, we will explore the process of identifying your target audience and understanding their needs and preferences. Social media platforms offer a wealth of data and insights that can help you identify and segment your audience effectively. By tailoring your content to resonate with your target audience, you can maximize engagement and drive meaningful interactions.

Once you have identified your target audience, we will dive into the various social media platforms and their unique features. From Facebook and Instagram to Twitter and LinkedIn, each platform offers different opportunities to engage with your audience. We will discuss the best practices for each platform and how to optimize your content to maximize reach and engagement.

Furthermore, we will explore the importance of monitoring and analyzing your social media metrics. By tracking key performance indicators (KPIs) such as reach, engagement, and conversion rates, you can gain valuable insights into the effectiveness of your social media marketing efforts. This data will help you identify areas for improvement and refine your strategy to achieve better results.

Lastly, we will emphasize the iterative nature of social media marketing. The digital landscape is constantly evolving, and it is crucial to adapt and refine your strategies

the knowledge and tools to create successful social media marketing campaigns that drive results for your business. Whether you are a marketing professional or someone new to the field, this subchapter will serve as a comprehensive guide to mastering social media marketing and achieving success in today's digital landscape.

accordingly. By staying updated with the latest trends and consumer behaviors, you can ensure that your social media marketing plans remain relevant and effective.

In conclusion, implementing and iterating social media marketing plans requires careful planning, audience understanding, platform optimization, and continuous monitoring. By following the strategies outlined in this subchapter, you will be equipped with

CONTINUOUS LEARNING AND STAYING UPDATED

In the rapidly evolving landscape of social media marketing, staying ahead of the curve is essential for anyone in the field of marketing and advertising. As platforms, algorithms, and consumer behavior constantly change, being proactive in your learning and staying updated is crucial to your success. This subchapter will explore the importance of continuous learning in social media marketing and provide strategies for staying updated in this ever-changing industry.

Why is continuous learning important in social media marketing? The answer lies in the dynamic nature of social media platforms and their algorithms. What works today may not work tomorrow, and what is trendy now may become outdated in a matter of weeks. By committing to continuous learning, you

ensure that your strategies remain relevant and effective

One of the most effective ways to stay updated in social media marketing is by following industry experts and thought leaders. These individuals are often at the forefront of new trends and developments. Engaging with their content, attending conferences, and participating in webinars and workshops can provide invaluable insights and keep you informed about the latest strategies and best practices.

Another strategy for continuous learning is to join professional communities and networking groups. These communities allow you to connect with like-minded professionals who share their experiences, insights, and knowledge. By participating actively in these communities,

you can gain a broader perspective and access to a wealth of information.

Additionally, taking online courses and certifications in social media marketing can help you stay updated and enhance your skills. Many reputable platforms offer courses specifically designed for marketers and advertisers, covering topics such as social media advertising, content creation, and analytics. These courses often provide practical knowledge and real-world examples that can be directly applied to your work.

Lastly, it is essential to stay informed about the latest updates and changes in social media platforms. Following official blogs, attending platform-specific webinars, and subscribing to newsletters can keep you up to date with algorithm changes, new features, and emerging trends. This knowledge will enable you to adapt your strategies accordingly and maintain a competitive edge.

In conclusion, continuous learning and staying updated are paramount in the field of social media marketing. By embracing a mindset of lifelong learning and utilizing various strategies such as following industry experts, joining professional communities, taking online courses, and staying informed about platform updates, you can ensure your success in this ever-evolving industry. Embrace the concept of continuous learning, and you will remain at the forefront of social media marketing strategies and achieve success in your marketing and advertising endeavors.

SUCCESS STORIES AND CASE STUDIES

In the fast-paced world of social media marketing, it's essential to stay ahead of the curve and learn from the successes and failures of others. This subchapter, "Success Stories and Case Studies," aims to provide you, anyone in

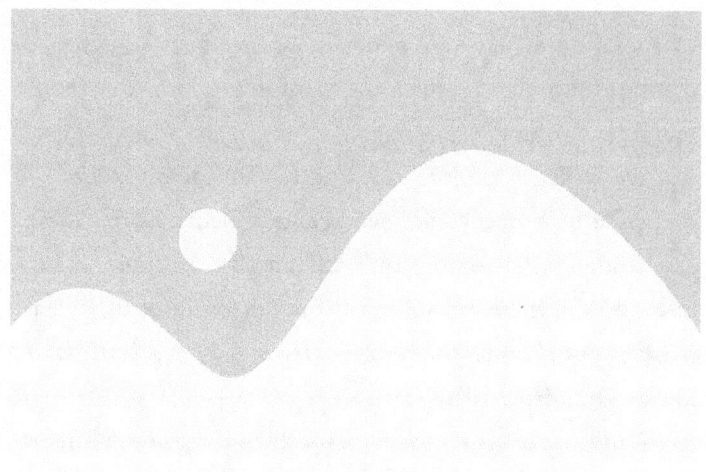

marketing and/or advertising, with real-life examples of how social media marketing can lead to outstanding results. By exploring these success stories and case studies, you will gain valuable insights and strategies for success in the ever-evolving field of social media marketing.

Within the realm of social media marketing, success stories abound, showcasing the power of engaging content, targeted campaigns, and creative strategies. We will delve into the success stories of various brands from different niches, highlighting how they effectively utilized social media platforms to achieve measurable results.

One such success story is the journey of XYZ Corporation, a global consumer goods company that effectively leveraged social media to launch a new product line. By employing a combination of visually appealing content, Influencer partnerships, and interactive campaigns, XYZ

Corporation managed to generate massive buzz and engagement, resulting in a significant boost in product sales and brand recognition.

We will also explore case studies focusing on niches such as fashion, food and beverage, travel, and more. These case studies will provide you with practical examples of how businesses in these niches successfully utilized social media marketing to connect with their target audience, build brand loyalty, and drive sales.

Additionally, this subchapter will emphasize the importance of analyzing and learning from both success stories and failures. By examining case studies of campaigns that did not achieve the desired results, you will gain a deeper understanding of the potential pitfalls and challenges that can arise in social media marketing. This knowledge will enable you to fine-tune your strategies and avoid common mistakes, ultimately increasing your chances of success.

With the ever-increasing popularity and influence of social media, it is vital for marketers and advertisers to stay informed and adaptable. By studying success stories and case studies, you will uncover innovative techniques, trends, and strategies that can help you excel in the dynamic world of social media marketing.

In conclusion, this subchapter on "Success Stories and Case Studies" aims to provide you, anyone in marketing and/or advertising, with a comprehensive overview of how social media marketing has been successfully implemented across various niches. By learning from the triumphs and failures of others, you will be better equipped to navigate the ever-changing landscape of social media marketing and achieve your own success.

FINAL WORDS AND ENCOURAGEMENT
FOR SOCIAL MEDIA MARKETERS

Congratulations! You have reached the end of The Ultimate Guide to Social Media Marketing: Strategies for Success. Throughout this book, we have explored the dynamic world of social media marketing and uncovered the strategies that can help you achieve remarkable success in this ever-evolving field. As you embark on your journey as a social media marketer, we would like to leave you with some final words of wisdom and encouragement.

First and foremost, always remember that social media marketing is not just about selling products or promoting services. It is about building meaningful connections with your audience, engaging with them, and providing them with valuable content. Social media platforms offer you a unique opportunity to showcase your brand's personality, values, and authenticity. Embrace this opportunity and create content that resonates with your target audience.

Keep in mind that social media algorithms are constantly changing. What works today may not work tomorrow. Stay updated with the latest trends and adapt your strategies accordingly. Experiment with different formats, such as videos, live streams, stories, and interactive content, to keep your audience engaged and interested.

Consistency is key in social media marketing. Develop a content calendar and stick to it. Regularly post high-quality content that aligns with your brand's voice and values. Engage with your audience by responding to comments, messages, and mentions. Building a loyal community requires time and effort, but the rewards are worth it.

Don't be afraid to take risks and think outside the box. Social media is a crowded space, and to stand out, you need to be creative and innovative. Experiment with new features, collaborate with influencers, and explore unconventional marketing strategies. Dare to be different and let your brand shine.

Remember that social media marketing is not a one-way street. Listen to your audience and learn from their feedback. Use analytics tools to track your performance and make data-driven decisions. Continuously monitor your social media channels and adapt your strategies based on the insights you gather.

Finally, never stop learning. Social media marketing is a rapidly evolving field, and the only way to stay ahead is by staying informed. Attend industry conferences, participate in webinars, read books, and follow thought leaders in the field. Stay curious and hungry for knowledge.

As you embark on your social media marketing journey, always remember that success takes time, dedication, and perseverance. It won't happen overnight, but with the right strategies and a genuine passion for your brand, you can achieve remarkable results. Embrace the challenges, learn from your mistakes, and celebrate your victories. The world of social media marketing is waiting for you to make your mark. Good luck!

BACK PAGE TITLE

Lorem Ipsum is simply dummy text of the printing and typesetting industry. Lorem Ipsum has been the industry's standard dummy text ever since the

s, when an unknown printer took a galley of type and scrambled it to make a type specimen book. It has survived not only ve centuries, but also the leap into electronic type-setting, remaining essentially unchanged. It was popularised in the s with the release of Letraset sheets containing Lorem Ipsum passages, and more recently with desktop publishing software like Aldus PageMaker including versions of Lorem Ipsum.